The Big Book of
DINOSAURS

Text by Dr. Ian Jenkins
Illustrated by Adrian Chesterman

...blishing
...f Zenith Entertainment plc
...set Street
...'U 7NA

Created by
act-two
346 Old Street
London EC1V 9RB

Text: Dr. Ian Jenkins, University of Bristol
Consultant: Professor Michael Benton, University of Bristol

Editor: Jacqueline McCann
Senior desginer: Helen Holmes
Art director: Belinda Webster
Main illustrations: Adrian Chesterman
Cartoon illustrations: Geo Parkin
Picture research: Daffydd Bynon & Jenny West
Pre-press production: Adam Wilde

First published by Two-Can Publishing in 2000

Copyright © 2002, 2000 Two-Can Publishing

HB ISBN 1-85434-846-9
PB ISBN 1-84301-045-3

Dewey Decimal Classification 567.9

HB 10 9 8 7 6 5 4 3 2 1
PB 10 9 8 7 6 5 4 3 2 1

A catalogue record for this book is available
from the British Library.

Photographic credits
page 4: Planet Earth Pictures, page 6:
Bruce Coleman, page 14: Natural History
Museum, London, page 19: Robert Wright/
Denver Museum Of Natural History, page 23:
Daniel Heuclin/Natural History Photographic
Agency, page 32: Natural History Museum,
London, page 35: Logan & Rota/American Museum
of Natural History, page 37: Oxford Scientific Films/
Earth Scenes, pages 40 & 42: Science Photo Library,
page 45: Tony Stone Images

Reproduction by Colourscan, Singapore
Printed by Graficromo, Spain

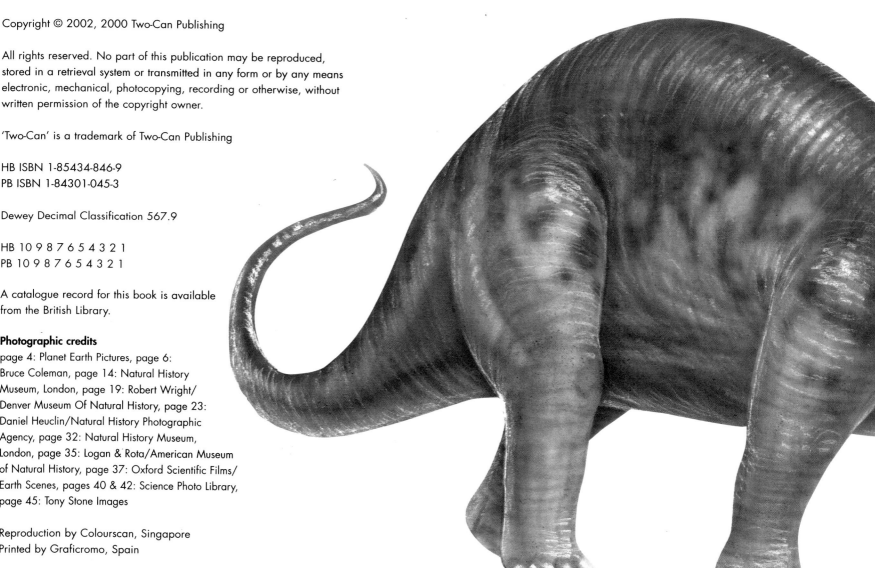

CONTENTS

Words that appear in bold in the text are explained here.

Find out how to pronounce the names of the dinosaurs here.

What is a dinosaur?

Dinosaurs were a group of prehistoric **reptiles** that first walked the Earth about 230 million years ago. These incredible creatures came in all shapes and sizes. Some were the height of a five-storey building and others were as small as a kitten. Dinosaurs were similar to modern reptiles because they lived on land, had scaly skin and laid eggs in nests.

Iguana
Today's reptiles, such as this iguana, walk with their legs sprawled outwards from their bodies. Dinosaurs walked with their legs tucked underneath their bodies.

Terrible reptiles

Dinosaur remains were first discovered in England, during the 1820s. One of the earliest palaeontologists was a man named Sir Richard Owen. He came across the fossilized bones of some huge, strange, ancient reptiles. Sir Richard named these reptiles after the ancient Greek words, 'deinos' and 'sauros', which together mean 'terrible reptile'.

How we know

We learn about dinosaurs by looking at their preserved bones, which are called **fossils**. Scientists who study fossilized bones are called **palaeontologists**. When palaeontologists find dinosaur fossils, they dig them up and take them to museums to study. To build up a picture of a whole creature, scientists piece together the fossil bones, just like a jigsaw puzzle. This can take many years and often there are pieces missing.

Iguanodon
Scientists have built a complete skeleton of the plant-eating dinosaur, *Iguanodon*.

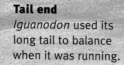

Tail end
Iguanodon used its long tail to balance when it was running.

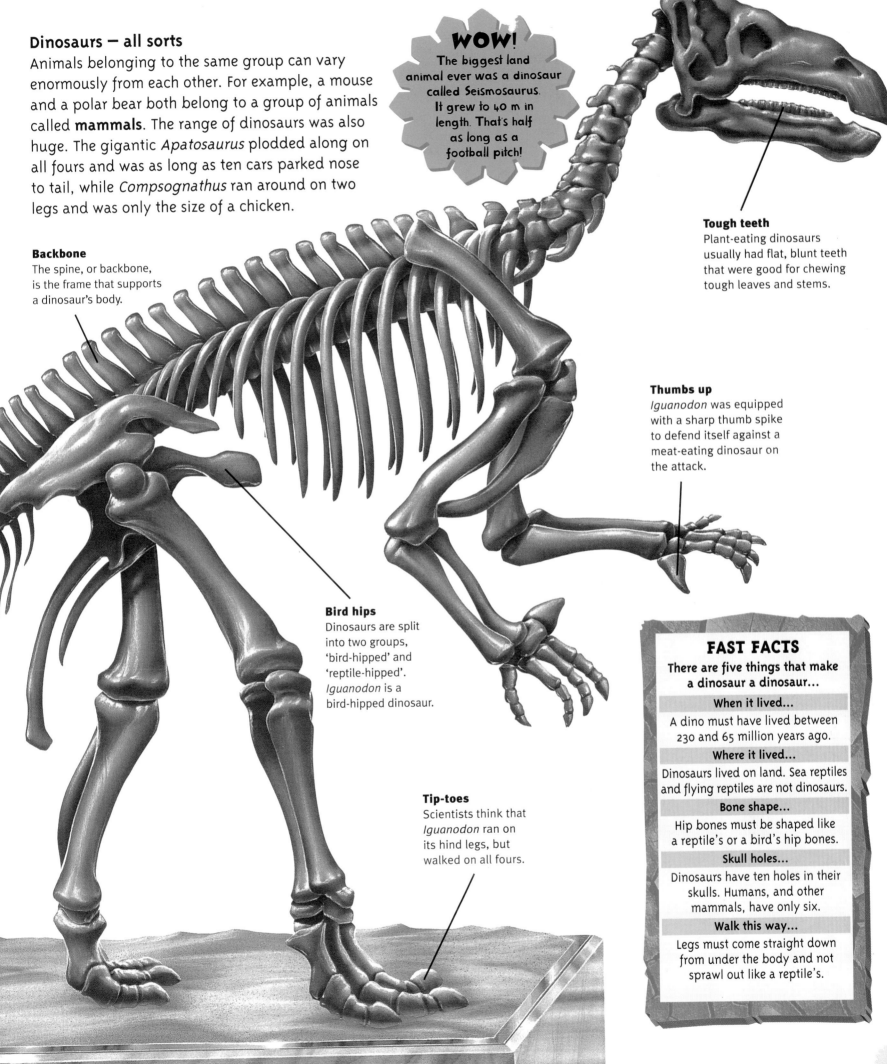

Dinosaurs — all sorts

Animals belonging to the same group can vary enormously from each other. For example, a mouse and a polar bear both belong to a group of animals called **mammals**. The range of dinosaurs was also huge. The gigantic *Apatosaurus* plodded along on all fours and was as long as ten cars parked nose to tail, while *Compsognathus* ran around on two legs and was only the size of a chicken.

WOW!
The biggest land animal ever was a dinosaur called Seismosaurus. It grew to 40 m in length. That's half as long as a football pitch!

Backbone
The spine, or backbone, is the frame that supports a dinosaur's body.

Tough teeth
Plant-eating dinosaurs usually had flat, blunt teeth that were good for chewing tough leaves and stems.

Thumbs up
Iguanodon was equipped with a sharp thumb spike to defend itself against a meat-eating dinosaur on the attack.

Bird hips
Dinosaurs are split into two groups, 'bird-hipped' and 'reptile-hipped'. *Iguanodon* is a bird-hipped dinosaur.

Tip-toes
Scientists think that *Iguanodon* ran on its hind legs, but walked on all fours.

FAST FACTS
There are five things that make a dinosaur a dinosaur...

When it lived...
A dino must have lived between 230 and 65 million years ago.

Where it lived...
Dinosaurs lived on land. Sea reptiles and flying reptiles are not dinosaurs.

Bone shape...
Hip bones must be shaped like a reptile's or a bird's hip bones.

Skull holes...
Dinosaurs have ten holes in their skulls. Humans, and other mammals, have only six.

Walk this way...
Legs must come straight down from under the body and not sprawl out like a reptile's.

Fossil finds

Fossils are the ancient remains of living things, locked in stone. Animal fossils can be anything from bones or teeth, to eggs or droppings. Even footprints, tracks and burrows can be fossilized. These are called trace fossils. **Palaeontologists** dig for all sorts of dinosaur fossils to try and uncover the amazing secrets of life on Earth millions of years ago.

▲ **Fossilized fish**
Palaeontologists have discovered the fossilized remains of fish, plants, insects and small sea creatures, as well as larger animals. This picture shows an ancient fish that swam in the sea over 150 million years ago.

How fossils form

The best fossils come from dinosaurs that died either in or near a river, swamp or ocean. Layers of mud and sand quickly cover the dinosaur, which helps to preserve the remains. Over millions of years, the dinosaur bones, and the layers of mud and sand around them, turn to stone. While this happens underground, lakes and rivers on the Earth's surface dry up, mountains form and new seas are born. A dinosaur that was buried under the sea, may reappear on a mountain top millions of years later!

▶ **These pictures show you how a dinosaur fossil forms.**

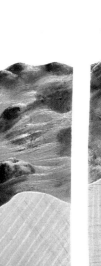

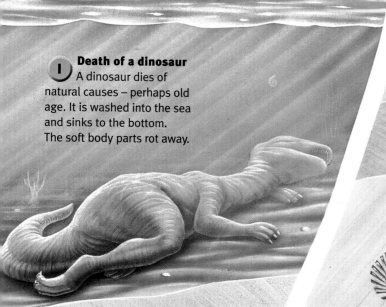

1 Death of a dinosaur
A dinosaur dies of natural causes – perhaps old age. It is washed into the sea and sinks to the bottom. The soft body parts rot away.

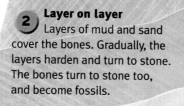

2 Layer on layer
Layers of mud and sand cover the bones. Gradually, the layers harden and turn to stone. The bones turn to stone too, and become fossils.

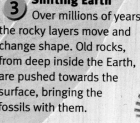

3 Shifting Earth
Over millions of years, the rocky layers move and change shape. Old rocks, from deep inside the Earth, are pushed towards the surface, bringing the fossils with them.

Detective work

Palaeontologists can find out all kinds of things by looking at fossils. By examining a dinosaur's teeth, a scientist can tell if the creature ate meat or plants. Sharp teeth tell us that the dinosaur was a meat-eater. Blunt teeth show that it liked chewing plants. When the contents of a dinosaur's stomach have been preserved, we can uncover vital clues about the dinosaur's diet and last meal.

4 **Exposed fossils**
At the surface, the weather wears away the rock around the fossils, leaving them uncovered. Dinosaur experts dig up the fossils.

Fossils on the move

It's hard to imagine, but millions of years ago, all the land on Earth was joined together in one huge **continent**. Over time, the continents have slowly moved. Today, when palaeontologists dig up dinosaur fossils, they know that the fossils have been carried thousands of miles away from where the dinosaur lived.

THE CHANGING WORLD

About 210 million years ago, all the continents were joined into one giant supercontinent, called **Pangaea**. Dinosaurs walked all over the Earth, without having to cross seas.

Plateosaurus lived where Germany and South Africa are today.

Around 120 million years ago, the land started to split up and drift apart. New continents and seas formed. The dinosaurs couldn't spread out as easily as before.

Iguanodon lived in what is now North America, Europe and Asia. The sea stopped *Iguanodon* from moving south.

Now, there are seven continents. Dinosaur fossils that are dug up today formed thousands of miles away and at a time when the Earth looked completely different.

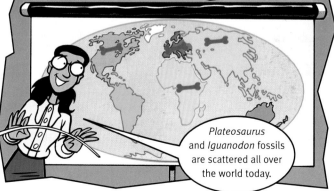

Plateosaurus and *Iguanodon* fossils are scattered all over the world today.

7

Dinosaur history

There are over 700 different types of dinosaurs and there may be many more we haven't discovered yet. Scientists have divided the dinosaurs into groups, based on the shape of their bones, the kind of food they ate, or the way they looked. To make the groups easy to understand, scientists often draw a dinosaur family tree.

ORNITHISCHIANS

'Bird-hipped' dinosaurs were all plant-eaters. This group split into five smaller groups.

227 million years ago

200-65 million years ago

Dinosaur groups

The first dinosaurs appeared 230 million years ago. **Palaeontologists** divide the early dinosaurs into two groups: those with bird hips and those with **reptile** hips. Within these groups, there are seven smaller dinosaur groups that share special features. Some have armour plates, others are giants and others have horns, or feet similar to birds. All dinosaurs belong to one of these seven groups.

▼ **Life on Earth**
Life on Earth began in the sea 3,000 million years ago. Gradually, the first simple creatures developed into animals. Eventually, animals moved on to the land and breathed air. After many millions of years, the dinosaurs appeared.

ORNITHOPODS

Some 'bird feet' dinosaurs walked on two legs and others walked on four. This group includes the duck-billed dinosaurs.

STEGOSAURS

'Roof reptiles' were large dinosaurs with spikes and plates on their bodies. They walked on four legs.

ANKYLOSAURS

'Fused reptiles' walked on all fours. Ankylosaurs were covered with heavy, protective body armour.

4,500 million years ago, the Earth was a fiery ball of liquid rock. Eventually, the Earth cooled down. The land, sea and **atmosphere** began to form.

3,000 million years ago, the first tiny signs of life appeared in the sea. Millions of years later, jellyfish, worms and sponges slowly developed.

375 million years ago, fish-like creatures that breathed air moved from the sea on to the land. They were called **amphibians**.

320 million years ago, the first reptiles appeared. They had scaly skin and sprawling legs. The dinosaurs were a kind of reptile.

Dinosaur family tree

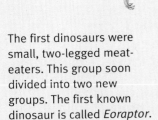

The first dinosaurs were small, two-legged meat-eaters. This group soon divided into two new groups. The first known dinosaur is called *Eoraptor*.

230 million years ago

SAURISCHIANS

'Reptile-hipped' dinosaurs ate meat or plants. Over millions of years, this group split into two smaller groups.

227 million years ago

200-65 million years ago

CERATOPSIANS

The 'horn faces' were four-legged dinosaurs. They had frills and horns on their heads.

PACHYCEPHALOSAURS

'Thick-headed reptiles' were dinosaurs with thick, bony heads. All the members of this family walked on two legs.

SAUROPODS

'Reptile feet' is the name given to the family of giant, long-necked, plant-eating dinosaurs. They walked on all fours.

THEROPODS

The 'beast feet' were all two-legged dinosaurs. Some theropods were enormous, others were tiny, but they all ate meat.

230 million years ago, the first dinosaurs walked the Earth. Early dinosaurs were human-sized. Later, they gave rise to all the dinosaur giants.

140 million years ago, birds and **mammals** first appeared. Eventually, they took over from the dinosaurs and ruled the land and sky.

65 million years ago, a **meteorite** may have hit the Earth. The dinosaurs died out. Some mammals, insects and other animals survived.

2 million years ago, the first humans walked upright. They made tools and used fire. Gradually, they learned how to communicate.

Reign of the dinosaurs

Dinosaurs lived on the planet for an incredible 165 million years. This period in Earth's history is called the **Mesozoic Era**. Scientists divide the era into three shorter timespans called the **Triassic**, **Jurassic** and **Cretaceous Periods**. During the Mesozoic Era, there were no ice-caps at the poles and the **climate** around the world was warm. Dinosaurs wandered freely all over the Earth.

WOW!
The first birds appeared during the Jurassic Period. Scientists say that birds today are just feathered dinosaurs with wings!

Triassic Period (250-205 million years ago)
During the Triassic, **Pangaea** was dominated by **reptiles**. The world then was very different to the world we live in today. The climate was hot and dry, and early plants such as horsetails, ferns and monkey puzzle trees covered the land. In the middle of the Triassic, the first dinosaurs appeared.

▽ Mussaurus

▲ Plateosaurus

▲ Herrerasaurus

Jurassic Period (205-145 million years ago)

The Jurassic world was much wetter than the Triassic. Pangaea was breaking up and the Atlantic Ocean began to form. The wind brought rain to dry areas which allowed more plants to grow. Tall pines, fern trees and low seed ferns provided lots of food for many dinosaurs.

▲ Diplodocus

◄ Allosaurus

Stegosaurus

Cretaceous Period (145-65 million years ago)

This period saw huge changes. The **continents** split into smaller pieces, seas flooded on to the land and volcanoes erupted. Dinosaurs fed on flowering plants, such as magnolias and roses, which appeared for the first time. Then, at the end of the Cretaceous, the dinosaurs mysteriously died out.

▼ Brachiosaurus

▲ Baryonyx

▶ Triceratops

Dino dining

The first dinosaurs were meat-eaters, or **carnivores**. A hungry carnivore, gobbled up anything it could catch and kill! Later, plant-eating dinosaurs, called **herbivores**, appeared. A large herbivore spent all day grazing and keeping a look-out for hungry carnivores on the prowl. Dinosaurs that ate a mixture of plants, insects and small **reptiles** are called **omnivores**.

DINO MENU
Feeling hungry? Check out some of these tasty dinosaur dishes...

CARNIVORE MENU
◆ speciality – freshly caught baby Mussaurus
◆ fish straight from the river
◆ fresh dino eggs
◆ rib of Plateosaurus
◆ assorted plate of dragonflies, beetles and centipedes
◆ plate of chopped lizard (other reptiles available)

HERBIVORE MENU
◆ speciality – mixed salad of cycad stems and ferns
◆ conifer needle salad
◆ fruit fool
◆ seed surprise

◀ Barosaurus

▼ Ceratosaurus

▼ Compsognathus

Food for thought
From the largest to the smallest, dinosaurs were constantly in search of food. *Barosaurus*, the 'heavy reptile', was a towering plant-eater that nipped off tonnes of leaves from tree tops every day. *Ceratosaurus* or 'horned reptile', preferred tearing into fresh meat. While 'pretty jaw', *Compsognathus*, a chicken-sized omnivore, scratched around for insects, seeds and anything else it could find.

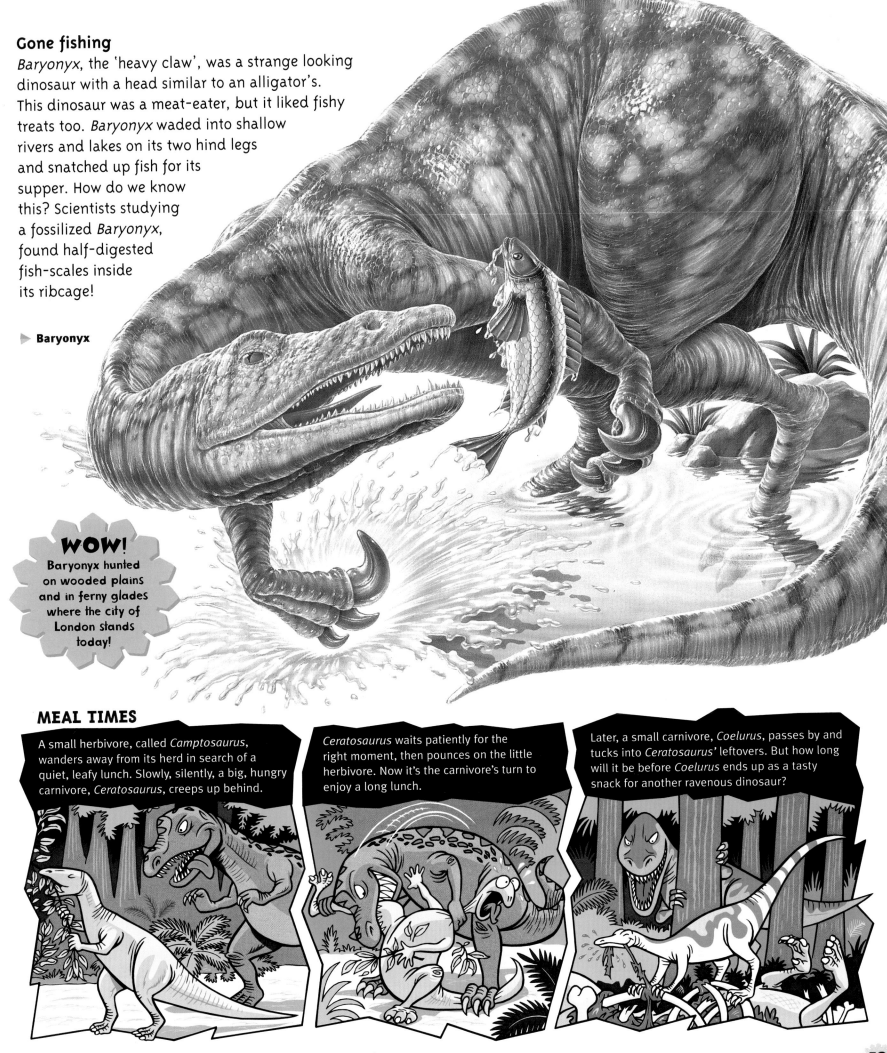

Gone fishing

Baryonyx, the 'heavy claw', was a strange looking dinosaur with a head similar to an alligator's. This dinosaur was a meat-eater, but it liked fishy treats too. *Baryonyx* waded into shallow rivers and lakes on its two hind legs and snatched up fish for its supper. How do we know this? Scientists studying a fossilized *Baryonyx*, found half-digested fish-scales inside its ribcage!

▶ **Baryonyx**

WOW!
Baryonyx hunted on wooded plains and in ferny glades where the city of London stands today!

MEAL TIMES

A small herbivore, called *Camptosaurus*, wanders away from its herd in search of a quiet, leafy lunch. Slowly, silently, a big, hungry carnivore, *Ceratosaurus*, creeps up behind.

Ceratosaurus waits patiently for the right moment, then pounces on the little herbivore. Now it's the carnivore's turn to enjoy a long lunch.

Later, a small carnivore, *Coelurus*, passes by and tucks into *Ceratosaurus'* leftovers. But how long will it be before *Coelurus* ends up as a tasty snack for another ravenous dinosaur?

Meat-eaters

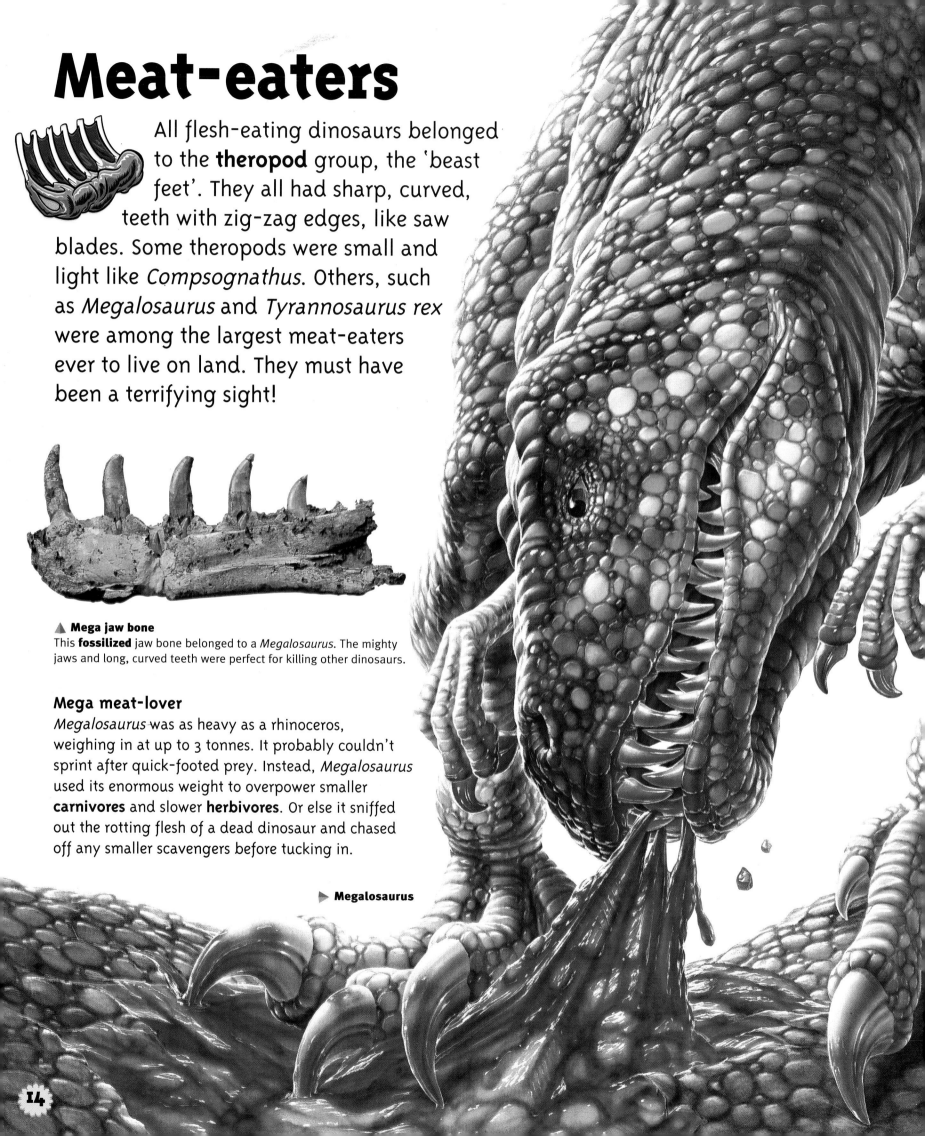

All flesh-eating dinosaurs belonged to the **theropod** group, the 'beast feet'. They all had sharp, curved, teeth with zig-zag edges, like saw blades. Some theropods were small and light like *Compsognathus*. Others, such as *Megalosaurus* and *Tyrannosaurus rex* were among the largest meat-eaters ever to live on land. They must have been a terrifying sight!

▲ **Mega jaw bone**
This **fossilized** jaw bone belonged to a *Megalosaurus*. The mighty jaws and long, curved teeth were perfect for killing other dinosaurs.

Mega meat-lover

Megalosaurus was as heavy as a rhinoceros, weighing in at up to 3 tonnes. It probably couldn't sprint after quick-footed prey. Instead, *Megalosaurus* used its enormous weight to overpower smaller **carnivores** and slower **herbivores**. Or else it sniffed out the rotting flesh of a dead dinosaur and chased off any smaller scavengers before tucking in.

▶ **Megalosaurus**

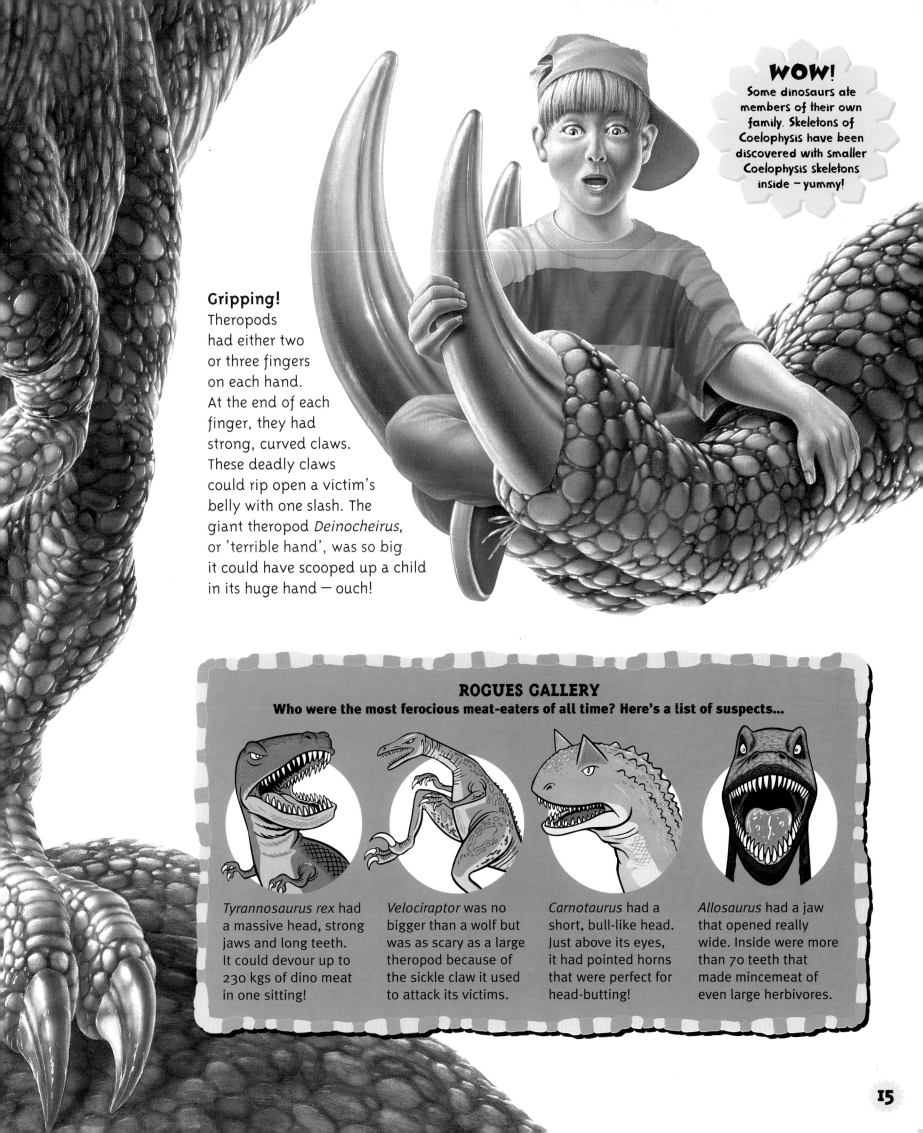

Gripping!

Theropods had either two or three fingers on each hand. At the end of each finger, they had strong, curved claws. These deadly claws could rip open a victim's belly with one slash. The giant theropod *Deinocheirus*, or 'terrible hand', was so big it could have scooped up a child in its huge hand — ouch!

ROGUES GALLERY
Who were the most ferocious meat-eaters of all time? Here's a list of suspects...

Tyrannosaurus rex had a massive head, strong jaws and long teeth. It could devour up to 230 kgs of dino meat in one sitting!

Velociraptor was no bigger than a wolf but was as scary as a large theropod because of the sickle claw it used to attack its victims.

Carnotaurus had a short, bull-like head. Just above its eyes, it had pointed horns that were perfect for head-butting!

Allosaurus had a jaw that opened really wide. Inside were more than 70 teeth that made mincemeat of even large herbivores.

Tyrannosaurus rex

Seventy million years ago, the most feared dinosaur of all was a giant **carnivore** called *Tyrannosaurus rex*, better known as *T. rex*. This beast, whose name means 'king of the tyrant **reptiles**', was one of the most powerful dinosaurs that ever lived. Although *T. rex* is the most famous of all the dinosaurs, only seven skeletons have been found in all. **Palaeontologists** dream of discovering the next one.

FAST FACTS

Dinosaur group	
Theropod	
When *Tyrannosaurus rex* lived	
Late Cretaceous — 70 mya	
Vital statistics	
Height 4.5 metres	
Length 12 metres	
Weight	
6.4 tonnes	
Fossils found	
North America	
Favourite snack	
Anything meaty — dead or alive!	
Worst enemy	
A bigger *T. rex*	

Horrible hunter

Tyrannosaurus rex was the last of all the hunting, or **predatory**, dinosaurs and one of the deadliest. This **theropod** had a gigantic body and a head as long as a man. Like *Megalosaurus*, *T. rex* wasn't built for sprinting, so it may have relied on surprise attacks. Hunting alone, or in pairs, *T. rex* tracked down its prey, targeting young, old or weak victims. On a good day, *T. rex* probably enjoyed a free meal when it came across a dead animal.

Gripping teeth
T. rex had about 60 razor-sharp teeth, each one 18 cm in length. That's almost 20 times longer than your teeth.

Mighty jaws
Tyrannosaurus rex had the heaviest skull and largest jaws of any theropod.

Thunder thighs
T. rex needed large leg bones and massive muscles to support its huge body.

Beady eyes
T. rex had tiny eyes for such a large dinosaur. Scientists think that it used its sense of smell, instead of sight, to find prey.

Giant meat-eaters rule

In 1902, when palaeontologists first discovered *T. rex*, they thought it was the biggest carnivore that had ever lived. But in 1995, in Argentina, scientists unearthed a bigger dinosaur, which they called *Giganotosaurus*. Then, in 1999, an even bigger flesh-eater was discovered. It hasn't been named yet, but this chap makes the other two look like small fry!

WOW!
The largest T. rex ever found was in 1990 in South Dakota, USA. The skeleton was sold to a museum in Chicago for a record $7.6 million!

Clever claws
On the end of each arm there were two fingers with claws as long as a man's hand.

Armed and dangerous
No one knows why *T. rex* had such short arms. They couldn't even reach its mouth. Scientists think that maybe *T. rex* used them to push up off the ground when it was lying down.

Plant-eaters

The **sauropods** were one of the most amazing groups of dinosaurs. These plant-eaters were so enormous that few **carnivores** dared to challenge them. A sauropod had a gigantic tail at one end, with a long neck and a tiny head at the other end. Because its mouth was so small, this gentle giant had to eat all day to keep its massive body well-fed.

▶ **Euhelopus**

Stone me!

Euhelopus, like most sauropods, ate tonnes of greenery every day. But with only short, peg-like front teeth, it was difficult for this giant to chew leathery leaves and tough plants. Scientists have worked out how the sauropods solved this problem. Many skeletons have been found with stones in their ribcages. *Euhelopus* and its relatives probably ate the stones, called **gastroliths**, to grind up the leafy food and make it easier to digest.

THWAP!

▶ **Mamenchisaurus**

Whiplash

Diplodocus was a sociable creature that travelled in herds. The large males protected the females and their young from prowling **theropods**, such as *Allosaurus*, which sneaked up on herds, trying to snatch a baby or a weak adult. But *Diplodocus* had a secret weapon — at the first sign of danger, it flicked its tail like a whip and knocked any **predator** for six!

Monster neck

Mamenchisaurus, a sauropod found in China, had the longest neck of any animal. At 15 metres long, you would think that this neck must have been heavy to carry around. Scientists studying **fossils** of *Mamenchisaurus'* neck bones have discovered that they were as thin as eggshell which means that its neck was much lighter than it looked.

Heavy weight

Diplodocus, the 'double beam', had a wavering neck, balanced by a long, tapering tail made of up to 80 bones. Without such a long tail, *Diplodocus* would have toppled over, head first!

▲ **Diplodocus**
The longest complete dinosaur skeleton found so far belongs to *Diplodocus*. At 27 metres long, this dinosaur was longer than a tennis court!

Apatosaurus

When *Apatosaurus* passed by, the ground trembled. This **sauropod** weighed about 80 tonnes, or as much as 16 elephants. Like all sauropods, *Apatosaurus* probably walked with its neck and tail held out from its body. Although *Apatosaurus* could lift its head to reach the tree tops, this **herbivore** preferred to graze on ferns, conifer trees and other juicy plants closer to the ground.

Leg work

It's difficult to believe, but **palaeontologists** think that *Apatosaurus* could stand up on its huge back legs. Scientists say that rearing up would have been a useful defence tactic. Even the toughest **theropod** would turn tail at the sight of this sauropod standing upright!

Thirsty work
When *Apatosaurus* stooped for a drink, it liked to feed on soft, water plants.

Long neck
This dinosaur's neck was so long that it could only support a small head at the end.

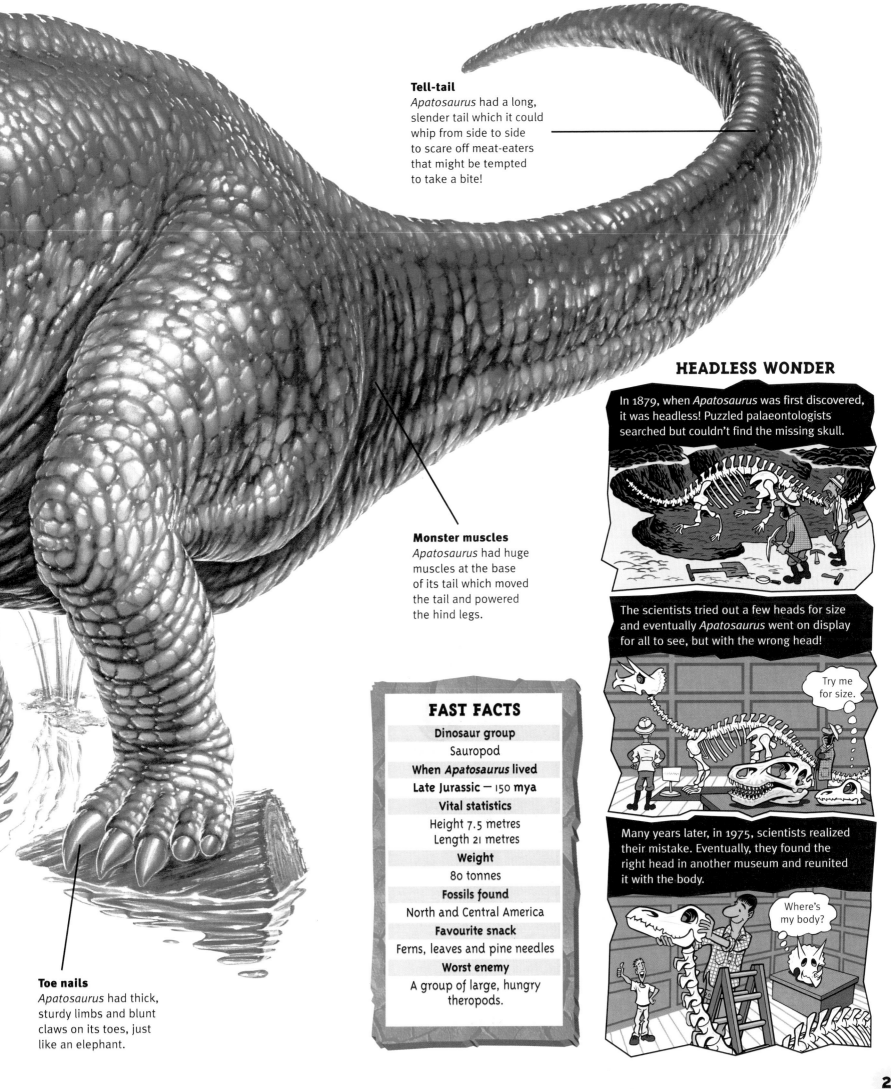

Tell-tail
Apatosaurus had a long, slender tail which it could whip from side to side to scare off meat-eaters that might be tempted to take a bite!

Monster muscles
Apatosaurus had huge muscles at the base of its tail which moved the tail and powered the hind legs.

Toe nails
Apatosaurus had thick, sturdy limbs and blunt claws on its toes, just like an elephant.

FAST FACTS

Dinosaur group
Sauropod

When *Apatosaurus* lived
Late Jurassic — 150 mya

Vital statistics
Height 7.5 metres
Length 21 metres

Weight
80 tonnes

Fossils found
North and Central America

Favourite snack
Ferns, leaves and pine needles

Worst enemy
A group of large, hungry theropods.

HEADLESS WONDER

In 1879, when *Apatosaurus* was first discovered, it was headless! Puzzled palaeontologists searched but couldn't find the missing skull.

The scientists tried out a few heads for size and eventually *Apatosaurus* went on display for all to see, but with the wrong head!

Try me for size.

Many years later, in 1975, scientists realized their mistake. Eventually, they found the right head in another museum and reunited it with the body.

Where's my body?

On the move

Dinosaurs spent most of the day on the move, looking for food, or escaping from **predators**. Fast-moving, two-legged **carnivores** lived alone, or in small groups. The **herbivores** lived in large herds roaming ferny plains and wooded forests in search of new grazing grounds. **Palaeontologists** think that some herbivores **migrated**, just as bison do today.

Footwork

Towards the end of the **Cretaceous Period**, there were more dinosaurs than at any other time. Some were built for speed, either to escape attackers or to chase prey. Others were heavy and slow. **Fossil** footprints tell us a lot about how dinosaurs moved. A single track of footprints tells us that a dinosaur was alone. A herd of animals left behind many sets of footprints.

Bagaceratops

These herbivores returned to the same place every year to build their nests. They wandered in large herds at a slow, steady pace.

Ornithomimus

The fastest dinosaurs were often the lightest. This two-legged **omnivore** raced along in small herds, at speeds of up to 32 km per hour.

Tarbosaurus

This **theropod** preferred to hunt alone. Its top speed was 12 km per hour which meant that swifter dinosaurs easily escaped its clutches.

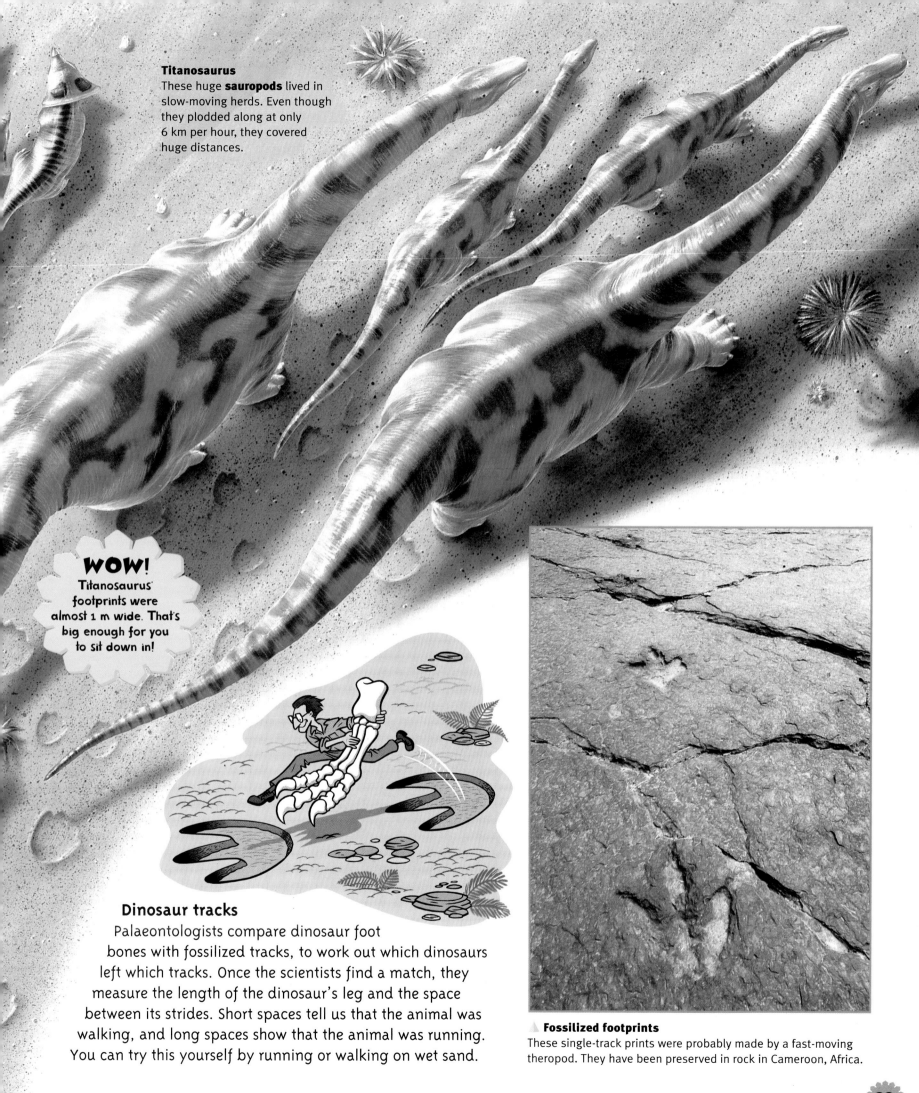

Titanosaurus
These huge **sauropods** lived in slow-moving herds. Even though they plodded along at only 6 km per hour, they covered huge distances.

WOW!
Titanosaurus' footprints were almost 1 m wide. That's big enough for you to sit down in!

Dinosaur tracks

Palaeontologists compare dinosaur foot bones with fossilized tracks, to work out which dinosaurs left which tracks. Once the scientists find a match, they measure the length of the dinosaur's leg and the space between its strides. Short spaces tell us that the animal was walking, and long spaces show that the animal was running. You can try this yourself by running or walking on wet sand.

Fossilized footprints
These single-track prints were probably made by a fast-moving theropod. They have been preserved in rock in Cameroon, Africa.

Struthiomimus

Struthiomimus was a dinosaur built for speed. At the first sign of danger, it broke into a sprint, taking long strides to escape the snapping jaws of a hungry **predator**. One of the fastest dinosaurs of all, this athletic **omnivore** had strong thigh muscles to power its long, slim legs. *Struthiomimus* needed to be quick because it didn't have horns, body armour or teeth to defend itself.

Twisting tail
To turn quickly, *Struthiomimus* held its tail out for balance and let it swing from side to side

Speedy Struthiomimus
Struthiomimus lived in small herds, galloping across low-lying plains. Unlike some of the slower dinosaurs, this bird-like dinosaur had large eyes which meant that it could see far and wide, so there was little chance of a surprise attack. *Struthiomimus* was nimble as well as speedy. With its short, compact body and strong, straight tail, it twisted and turned to escape dinosaurs that weren't so quick on their feet.

WOW!
Struthiomimus was as fast as a racehorse and it could easily have beaten an Olympic sprinter in a 100-metre race.

Leg power
Struthiomimus probably reached speeds of up to 40 km per hour.

Handy work
Nimble hands with three fingers and long claws made it easy to pick fruit or snap twigs from trees and bushes.

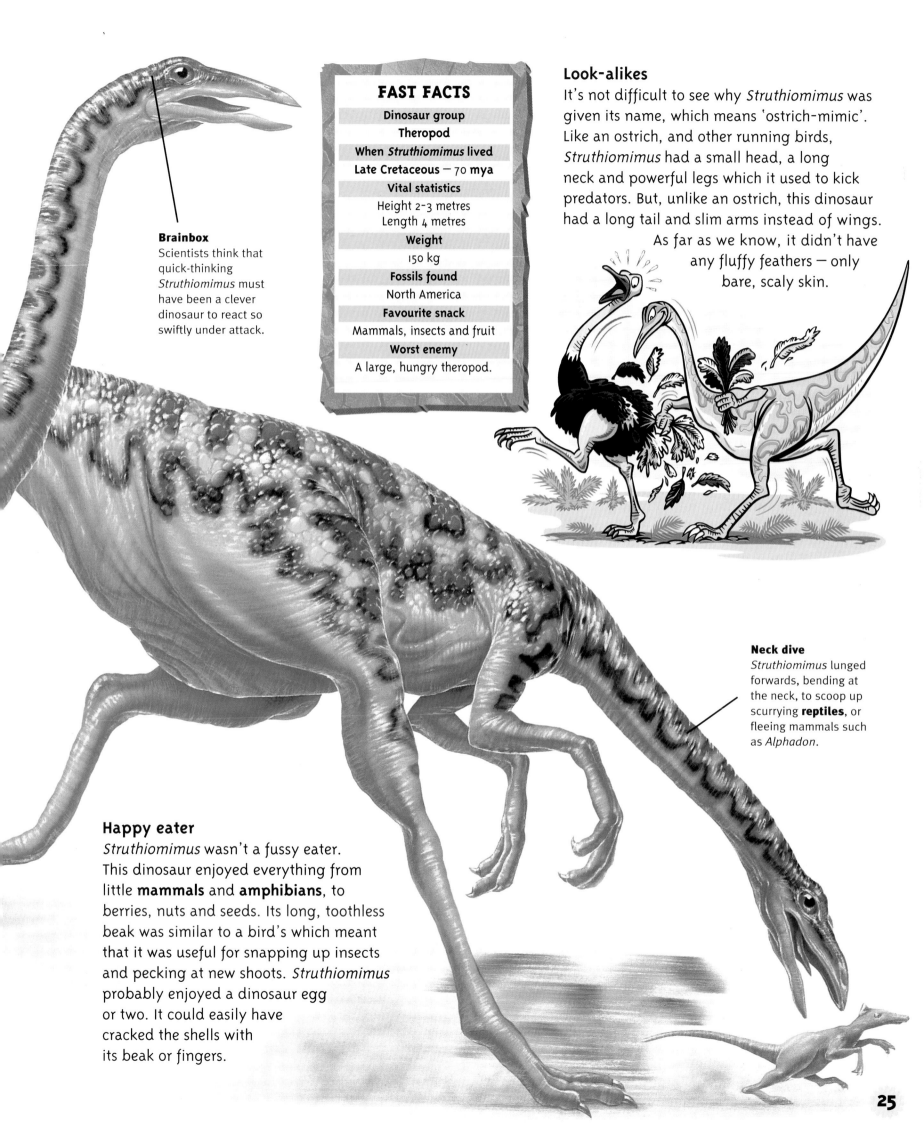

Brainbox
Scientists think that quick-thinking *Struthiomimus* must have been a clever dinosaur to react so swiftly under attack.

FAST FACTS

Dinosaur group	
Theropod	
When *Struthiomimus* lived	
Late Cretaceous — 70 mya	
Vital statistics	
Height 2–3 metres	
Length 4 metres	
Weight	
150 kg	
Fossils found	
North America	
Favourite snack	
Mammals, insects and fruit	
Worst enemy	
A large, hungry theropod.	

Look-alikes

It's not difficult to see why *Struthiomimus* was given its name, which means 'ostrich-mimic'. Like an ostrich, and other running birds, *Struthiomimus* had a small head, a long neck and powerful legs which it used to kick predators. But, unlike an ostrich, this dinosaur had a long tail and slim arms instead of wings. As far as we know, it didn't have any fluffy feathers — only bare, scaly skin.

Neck dive
Struthiomimus lunged forwards, bending at the neck, to scoop up scurrying **reptiles**, or fleeing mammals such as *Alphadon*.

Happy eater

Struthiomimus wasn't a fussy eater. This dinosaur enjoyed everything from little **mammals** and **amphibians**, to berries, nuts and seeds. Its long, toothless beak was similar to a bird's which meant that it was useful for snapping up insects and pecking at new shoots. *Struthiomimus* probably enjoyed a dinosaur egg or two. It could easily have cracked the shells with its beak or fingers.

Attack and defence

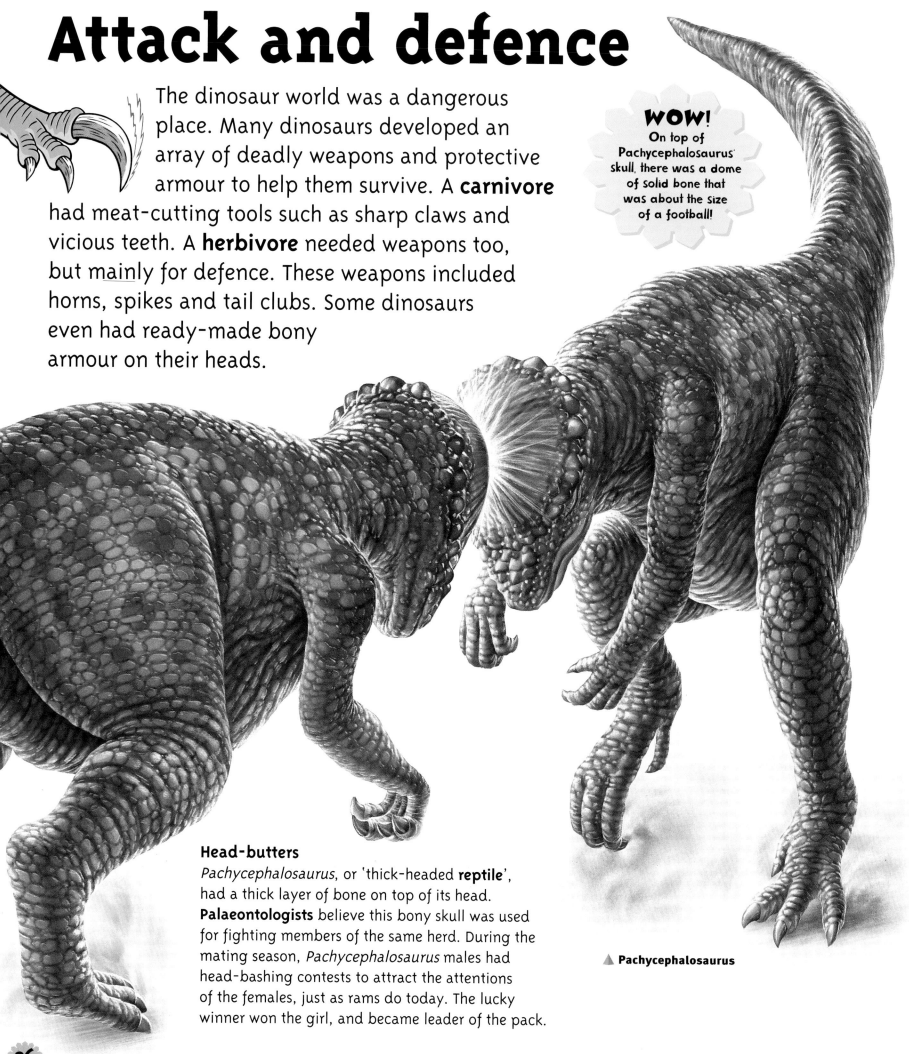

The dinosaur world was a dangerous place. Many dinosaurs developed an array of deadly weapons and protective armour to help them survive. A **carnivore** had meat-cutting tools such as sharp claws and vicious teeth. A **herbivore** needed weapons too, but mainly for defence. These weapons included horns, spikes and tail clubs. Some dinosaurs even had ready-made bony armour on their heads.

WOW!
On top of Pachycephalosaurus' skull, there was a dome of solid bone that was about the size of a football!

Head-butters

Pachycephalosaurus, or 'thick-headed **reptile**', had a thick layer of bone on top of its head. **Palaeontologists** believe this bony skull was used for fighting members of the same herd. During the mating season, *Pachycephalosaurus* males had head-bashing contests to attract the attentions of the females, just as rams do today. The lucky winner won the girl, and became leader of the pack.

▲ **Pachycephalosaurus**

Team work

Some of the most ferocious hunters were smaller than their prey. Small, fast **theropods**, such as *Deinonychus*, probably hunted in packs, knocking their victims to the ground, just as lions and cheetahs do. Good team work meant that they could kill a large **ornithopod** such as *Tenontosaurus* and share the meat. *Deinonychus*, the 'terrible claw', also had the help of a large sickle-shaped claw on its second toe.

▶ **Tenontosaurus**

▼ **Deinonychus**

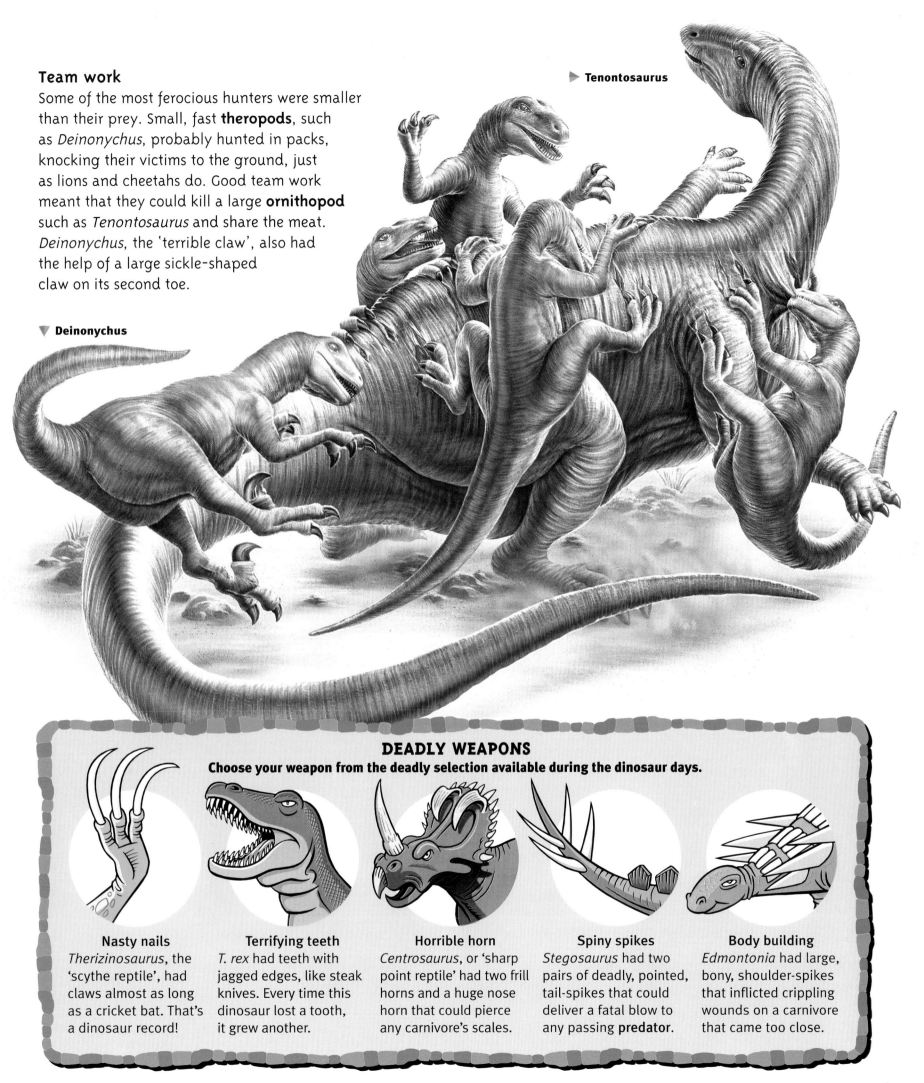

DEADLY WEAPONS

Choose your weapon from the deadly selection available during the dinosaur days.

Nasty nails
Therizinosaurus, the 'scythe reptile', had claws almost as long as a cricket bat. That's a dinosaur record!

Terrifying teeth
T. rex had teeth with jagged edges, like steak knives. Every time this dinosaur lost a tooth, it grew another.

Horrible horn
Centrosaurus, or 'sharp point reptile' had two frill horns and a huge nose horn that could pierce any carnivore's scales.

Spiny spikes
Stegosaurus had two pairs of deadly, pointed, tail-spikes that could deliver a fatal blow to any passing **predator**.

Body building
Edmontonia had large, bony, shoulder-spikes that inflicted crippling wounds on a carnivore that came too close.

Stegosaurus

Stegosaurus, the 'roof **reptile**', was a remarkable looking dinosaur, with massive protective plates sticking out of its back and sharp spikes at the end of its tail. For a dinosaur of its size, *Stegosaurus* had a surprisingly small head with a little beak at the tip of its snout. Like the **sauropods**, this **herbivore** spent most of its time chomping plants, trying to eat enough to feed its enormous body.

FAST FACTS

Dinosaur group	
Stegosaurs	
When *Stegosaurus* lived	
Late Jurassic — 160 **mya**	
Vital statistics	
Height 3 metres Length 9 metres	
Weight	
2 tonnes	
Fossils found	
North America	
Favourite snack	
Leaves, twigs and juicy plants	
Worst enemy	
Allosaurus or *Ceratosaurus*	

Back plates
Two rows of bony back plates ran from head to tail. The biggest plates were almost as big as you.

Solar panels
There are many theories about the plates on *Stegosaurus'* back. People used to think that they protected the dinosaur. Nowadays, scientists think the plates were part of a heating and cooling system. The plates soaked up heat from the Sun, like solar panels, and gave off heat in the shade. It's also possible that the plates were brightly coloured, to attract a mate. Or perhaps the males used them as a warning to other males to keep out of their territory!

Family ties
Scientists think that *Stegosaurus* probably recognized other members of its family by the shape and size of their back plates.

Tail spikes
When *Stegosaurus* came under attack, it swung its tail, lashing out with spikes that were as long as a baseball bat.

Balancing act
When *Stegosaurus* stood up, its back legs and tail made a triangle shape which helped it to balance.

Cheeky
This plant-lover had a small beak. Inside its cheeks were 150 small leaf-shaped teeth, for chewing tough plants.

WOW!
Stegosaurus' brain was only as big as a dog's, but its body was about 100 times bigger!

Aiming high

Many **palaeontologists** wonder why *Stegosaurus'* hind legs were so much longer than the front ones. This dinosaur grazed on ferns and cycad plants that lay close to the ground, in the way that cows and sheep do today. So why did it need long hind legs? Scientists think that *Stegosaurus* may have been able to stand up on its back legs and reach lush leaves high up. *Stegosaurus'* huge legs and flexible tail supported its enormous body as it stretched for food.

IDENTITY PARADE
Welcome to the stegosaur line-up. These dinosaurs are all members of the same family. Can you tell why?

Kentrosaurus, the 'spiky reptile' from Africa lived up to its name. A few smallish plates ran down its neck, followed by very long, pointed spines along its back.

Wuerhosaurus was named after Wuerho, the village in China where it was found. This dinosaur had small, blunt back-plates, with two, huge, curved tail spikes.

Tuojiangosaurus was named after the Tuo River in China. Its front legs were bent, a bit like a crocodile's, and its plates were sharply pointed at the top.

Armoured dinosaurs

Towards the end of the **Cretaceous Period** a new kind of armoured dinosaur, called the **ankylosaur**, or 'fused **reptile**', appeared. Some members of this family had spikes, others had tail clubs, but they all had one thing in common — bony plates that fitted together like a coat of armour over most of the body.
These tank-like **herbivores** were a challenge to even the most determined **carnivores**.

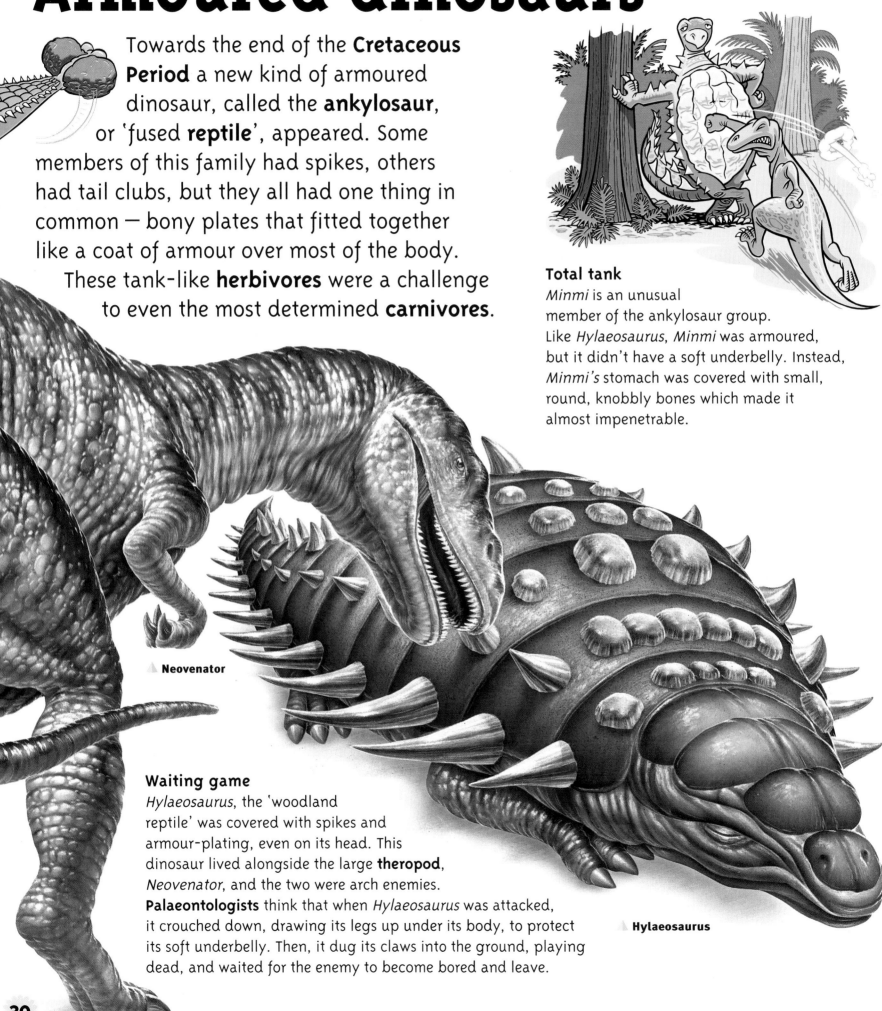

Total tank
Minmi is an unusual member of the ankylosaur group. Like *Hylaeosaurus*, *Minmi* was armoured, but it didn't have a soft underbelly. Instead, *Minmi's* stomach was covered with small, round, knobbly bones which made it almost impenetrable.

▲ **Neovenator**

Waiting game
Hylaeosaurus, the 'woodland reptile' was covered with spikes and armour-plating, even on its head. This dinosaur lived alongside the large **theropod**, *Neovenator*, and the two were arch enemies.
Palaeontologists think that when *Hylaeosaurus* was attacked, it crouched down, drawing its legs up under its body, to protect its soft underbelly. Then, it dug its claws into the ground, playing dead, and waited for the enemy to become bored and leave.

▲ **Hylaeosaurus**

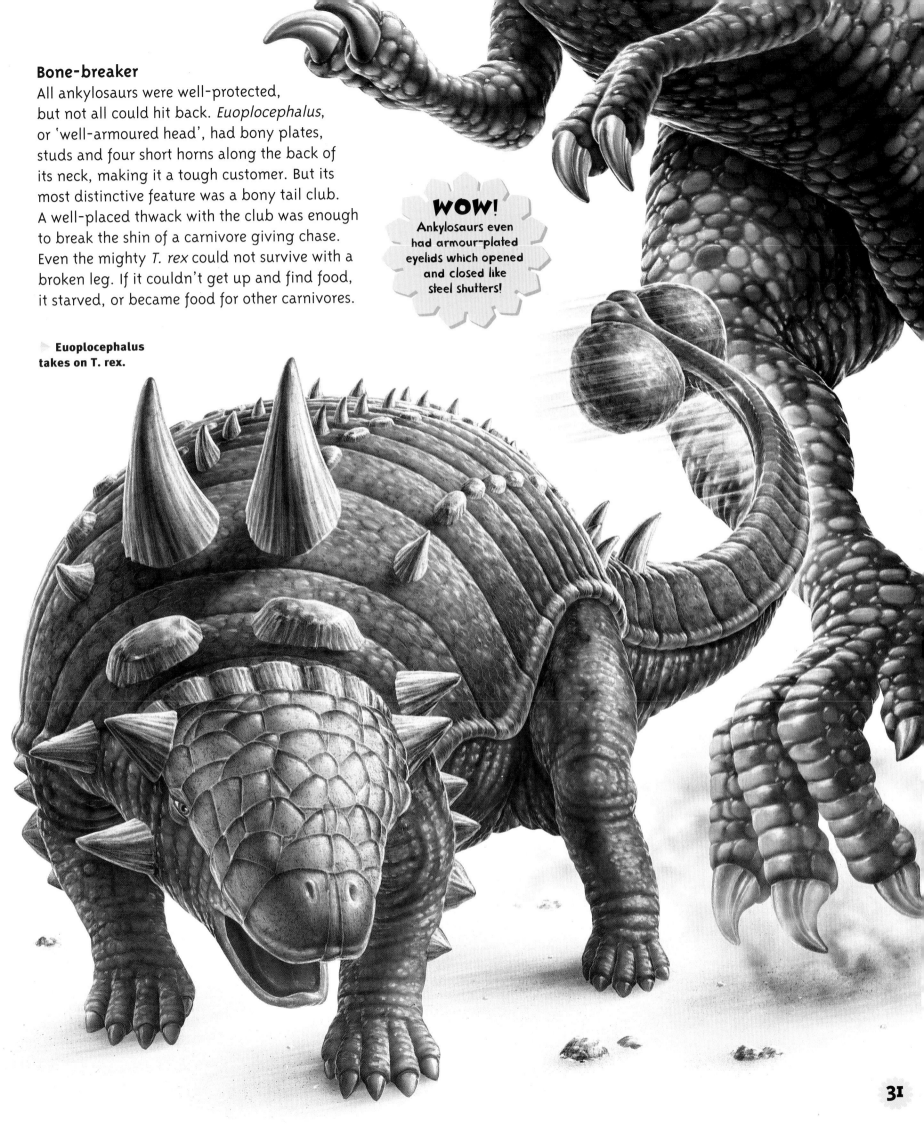

Bone-breaker

All ankylosaurs were well-protected, but not all could hit back. *Euoplocephalus*, or 'well-armoured head', had bony plates, studs and four short horns along the back of its neck, making it a tough customer. But its most distinctive feature was a bony tail club. A well-placed thwack with the club was enough to break the shin of a carnivore giving chase. Even the mighty *T. rex* could not survive with a broken leg. If it couldn't get up and find food, it starved, or became food for other carnivores.

▶ **Euoplocephalus takes on T. rex.**

WOW!
Ankylosaurs even had armour-plated eyelids which opened and closed like steel shutters!

Triceratops

Triceratops, or 'three-horned face', is the most famous member of the **ceratopsian** group. Small ceratopsians looked like pigs with horns, but a large one, such as *Triceratops*, was more like a frilled rhinoceros. These heavy **herbivores** lived in large herds, wandering through warm, breezy woodlands of North America.

Horns and frills

Triceratops' most striking features were its horns and frill. The bony frill protected the dinosaur's neck from the sharp teeth and claws of **theropods**. The horns came in useful when *Triceratops* was attacked. Then, it charged, head lowered, horns at the ready. The long brow horns inflicted fatal wounds when they pierced an enemy's skin. **Palaeontologists** also think that male *Triceratops* used their horns for wrestling one another, just as stags use their antlers today.

WOW!
The ceratopsian *Torosaurus* had the biggest skull of any land animal ever. The skull and frill together were 2.5 m long. That's longer than a small car!

▼ **Triceratops skeleton**
This **fossilized** skeleton of a *Triceratops* was found in Wyoming, USA. Most ceratopsians have holes in their bony frills, but *Triceratops'* frill was completely solid.

Feet first
Triceratops had four toes on its back feet and five on the front. The toes were stumpy and spread out slightly, to bear the weight of this heavy dinosaur.

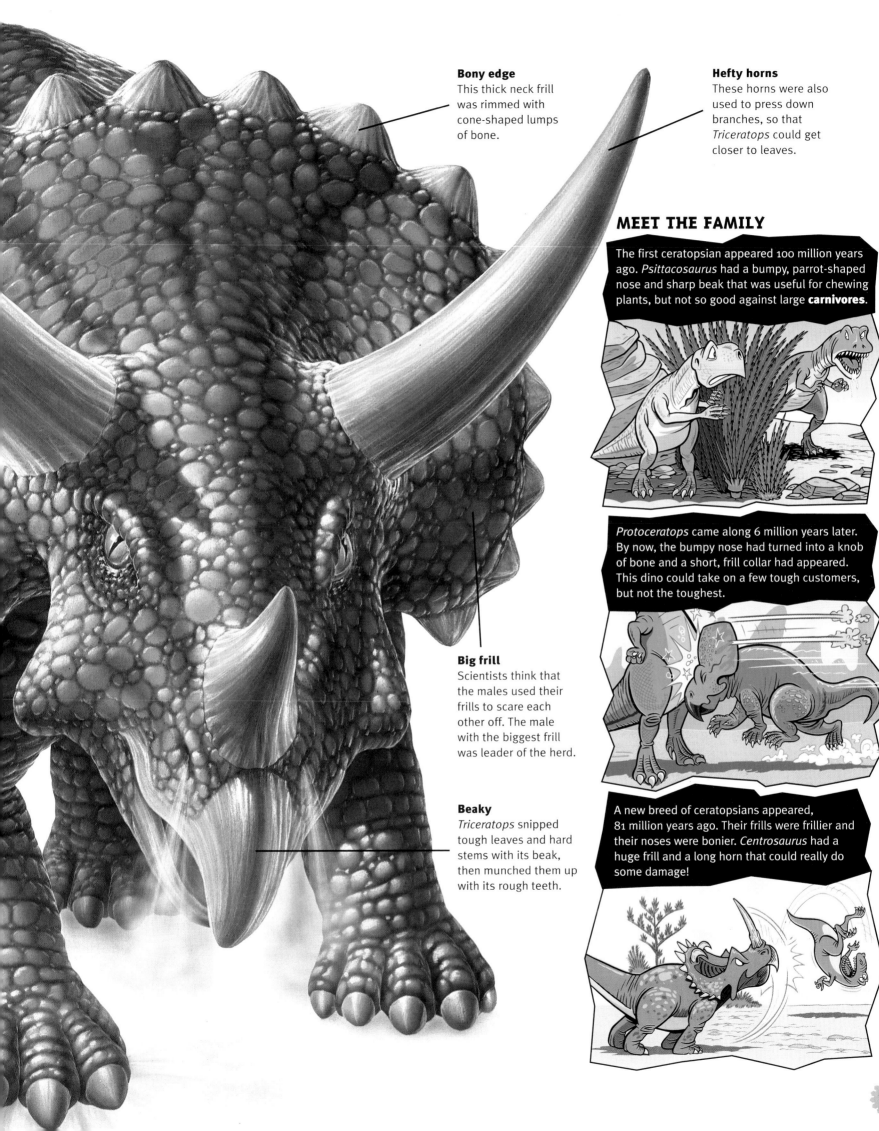

Bony edge
This thick neck frill was rimmed with cone-shaped lumps of bone.

Hefty horns
These horns were also used to press down branches, so that *Triceratops* could get closer to leaves.

MEET THE FAMILY

The first ceratopsian appeared 100 million years ago. *Psittacosaurus* had a bumpy, parrot-shaped nose and sharp beak that was useful for chewing plants, but not so good against large **carnivores**.

Protoceratops came along 6 million years later. By now, the bumpy nose had turned into a knob of bone and a short, frill collar had appeared. This dino could take on a few tough customers, but not the toughest.

A new breed of ceratopsians appeared, 81 million years ago. Their frills were frillier and their noses were bonier. *Centrosaurus* had a huge frill and a long horn that could really do some damage!

Big frill
Scientists think that the males used their frills to scare each other off. The male with the biggest frill was leader of the herd.

Beaky
Triceratops snipped tough leaves and hard stems with its beak, then munched them up with its rough teeth.

Corythosaurus

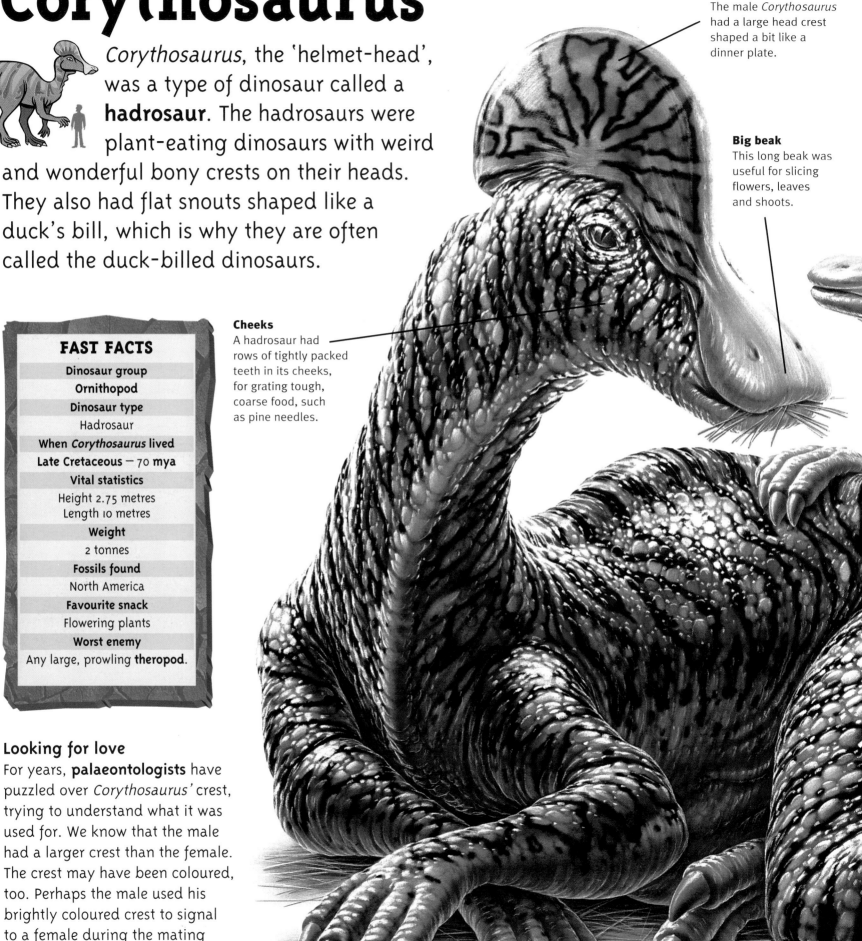

Corythosaurus, the 'helmet-head', was a type of dinosaur called a **hadrosaur**. The hadrosaurs were plant-eating dinosaurs with weird and wonderful bony crests on their heads. They also had flat snouts shaped like a duck's bill, which is why they are often called the duck-billed dinosaurs.

Colourful crest
The male *Corythosaurus* had a large head crest shaped a bit like a dinner plate.

Big beak
This long beak was useful for slicing flowers, leaves and shoots.

Cheeks
A hadrosaur had rows of tightly packed teeth in its cheeks, for grating tough, coarse food, such as pine needles.

FAST FACTS

Dinosaur group
Ornithopod

Dinosaur type
Hadrosaur

When *Corythosaurus* lived
Late Cretaceous – 70 **mya**

Vital statistics
Height 2.75 metres
Length 10 metres

Weight
2 tonnes

Fossils found
North America

Favourite snack
Flowering plants

Worst enemy
Any large, prowling **theropod**.

Looking for love

For years, **palaeontologists** have puzzled over *Corythosaurus'* crest, trying to understand what it was used for. We know that the male had a larger crest than the female. The crest may have been coloured, too. Perhaps the male used his brightly coloured crest to signal to a female during the mating season, just as some male birds use their bright feathers to attract females.

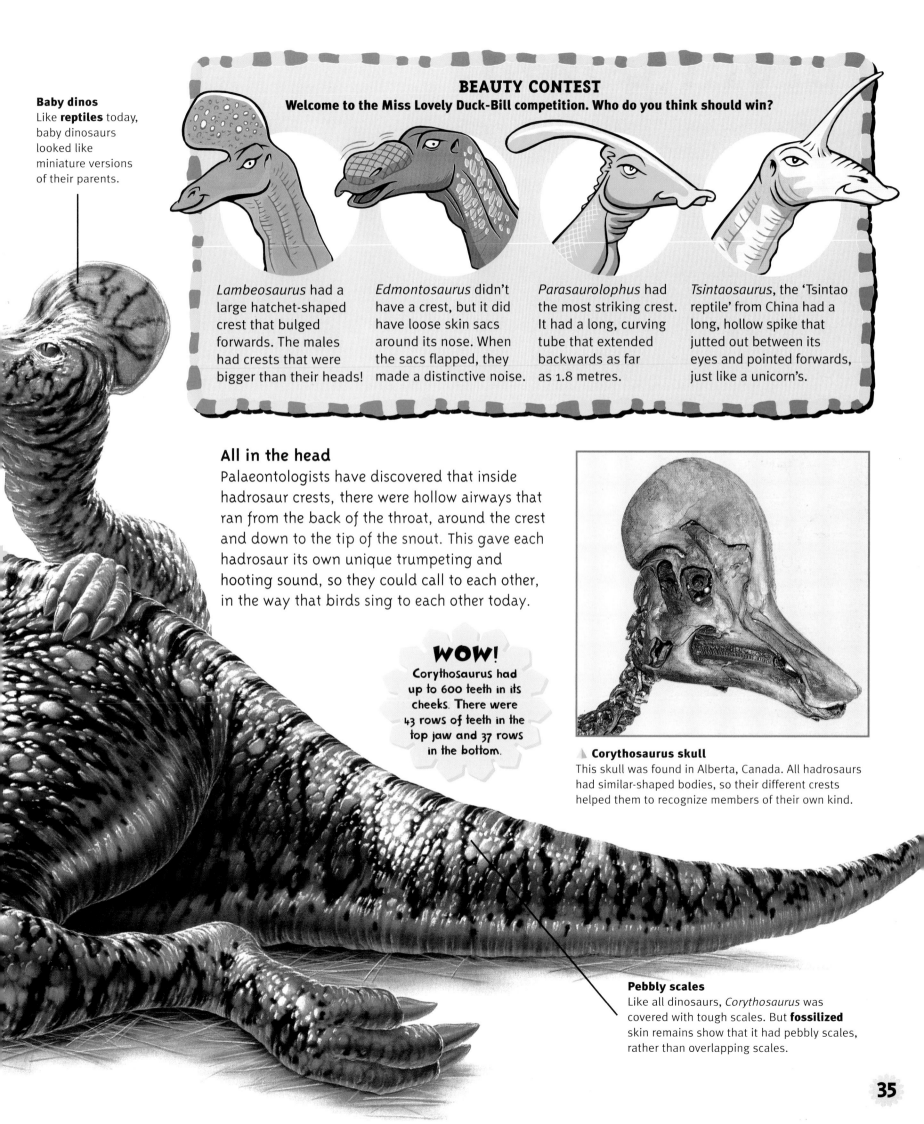

Baby dinos
Like **reptiles** today, baby dinosaurs looked like miniature versions of their parents.

BEAUTY CONTEST
Welcome to the Miss Lovely Duck-Bill competition. Who do you think should win?

Lambeosaurus had a large hatchet-shaped crest that bulged forwards. The males had crests that were bigger than their heads!

Edmontosaurus didn't have a crest, but it did have loose skin sacs around its nose. When the sacs flapped, they made a distinctive noise.

Parasaurolophus had the most striking crest. It had a long, curving tube that extended backwards as far as 1.8 metres.

Tsintaosaurus, the 'Tsintao reptile' from China had a long, hollow spike that jutted out between its eyes and pointed forwards, just like a unicorn's.

All in the head
Palaeontologists have discovered that inside hadrosaur crests, there were hollow airways that ran from the back of the throat, around the crest and down to the tip of the snout. This gave each hadrosaur its own unique trumpeting and hooting sound, so they could call to each other, in the way that birds sing to each other today.

WOW!
Corythosaurus had up to 600 teeth in its cheeks. There were 43 rows of teeth in the top jaw and 37 rows in the bottom.

▲ Corythosaurus skull
This skull was found in Alberta, Canada. All hadrosaurs had similar-shaped bodies, so their different crests helped them to recognize members of their own kind.

Pebbly scales
Like all dinosaurs, *Corythosaurus* was covered with tough scales. But **fossilized** skin remains show that it had pebbly scales, rather than overlapping scales.

Parent power

Dinosaur mothers laid their eggs in soft nests and kept the eggs safe until they hatched, just as birds do. Like baby birds, young dinosaurs were easy prey for **predators** and many didn't survive. Most dinosaur hatchlings had to look after themselves, although a few mothers watched over their babies until they became young adults.

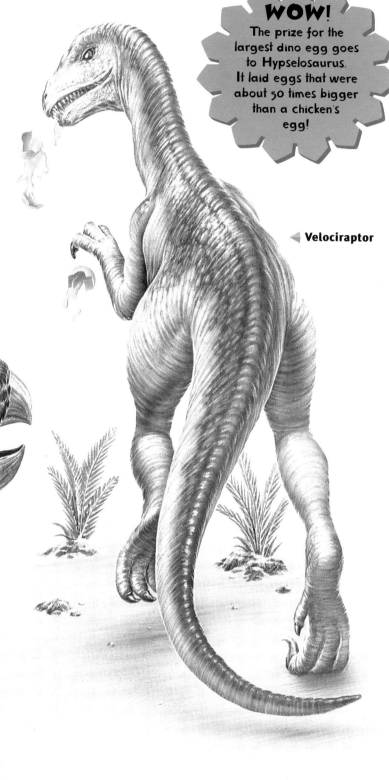

◀ **Velociraptor**

▲ **Protoceratops**

Protective parents

Protoceratops lived in dry, windswept deserts and every year, the females laid their eggs in sandy nests. The female *Protoceratops* was always on the look-out for **carnivores** in search of a quick snack. **Theropods**, such as *Velociraptor*, the 'quick thief', would sneak up to the nest and try to steal an egg or two, because they were full of goodness. If *Protoceratops* caught *Velociraptor*, the angry mother would tear the smaller dinosaur to pieces!

Maiasaura, the 'good-mother reptile'

Maiasaura was a duck-billed dinosaur that bred in large groups. Every year, the females trekked back to the same place to lay their eggs. A mother *Maiasaura* scooped out a huge nest in the mud, then laid about 20 eggs. When her babies hatched, *Maiasaura* looked after the hatchlings, bringing them juicy plants for a few months until they were strong enough to walk and find their own food.

▶ **Maiasaura**

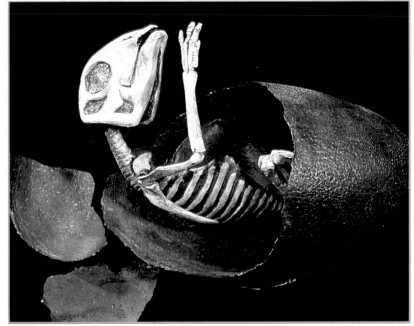

▲ **Captured in time**
This **fossilized** eggshell contains a hatchling *Maiasaura*. It was found in Montana, USA, with many other fossilized eggs and babies.

Facing the enemy

Dinosaur parents had a full-time job protecting their hatchlings from predators. When danger was near, *Chasmosaurus* parents herded their young together and formed a circle around them. The adults faced outwards, towards the enemy, showing their large horns and frills as a warning to any meat-eater that came too close.

Beasts of land and sky

Dinosaurs weren't the only animals to live millions of years ago. The land and sky were full of other prehistoric beasts. Strange **reptiles** stalked the Earth and small **mammals** took cover underground. Flying and soaring over-head in the **Mesozoic** skies, were strange creatures called **pterosaurs**, or 'flying reptiles'.

Reptiles and mammals
Huge reptiles walked the Earth long before the dinosaurs. One of the earliest, *Dimetrodon*, carried an impressive sail on its back. During the **Triassic Period**, another group of reptiles called the **thecodonts** appeared. One, *Desmatosuchus*, looked like a scary mix of dinosaur and crocodile. Early mammals, such as the shrew-like *Megazostrodon*, burrowed underground to escape fierce **predators**.

Dragons of the air
The pterosaurs were close relatives of the dinosaurs and they dominated the ancient skies. Some pterosaurs were no bigger than a sparrow, but others were like gigantic bats, flapping high in the sky. *Quetzalcoatlus*, or 'flying dragon', was the biggest flying creature of all time. Its wingspan was 11.5 metres — the size of a small aircraft.

▶ **Dimetrodon**

▲ **Megazostrodon**

▶ **Desmatosuchus**

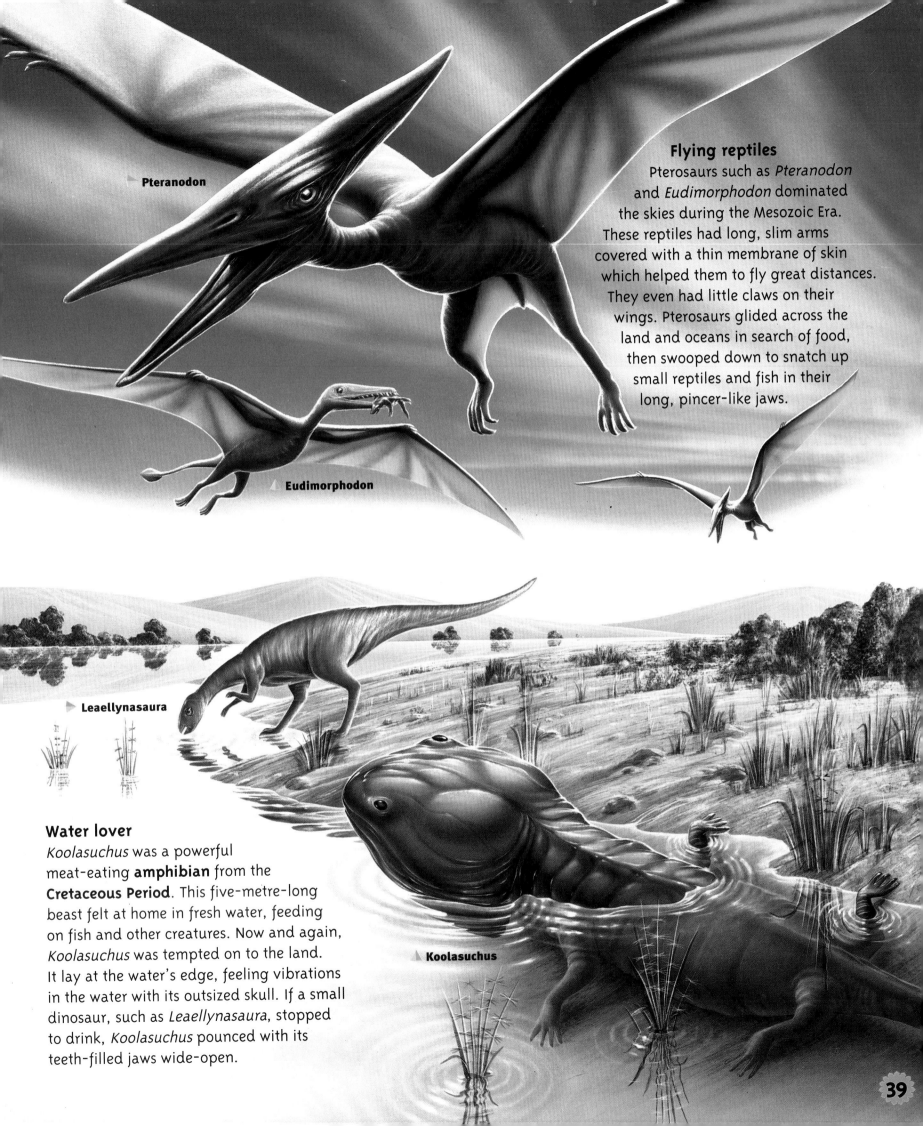

Pteranodon

Eudimorphodon

Flying reptiles
Pterosaurs such as *Pteranodon* and *Eudimorphodon* dominated the skies during the Mesozoic Era. These reptiles had long, slim arms covered with a thin membrane of skin which helped them to fly great distances. They even had little claws on their wings. Pterosaurs glided across the land and oceans in search of food, then swooped down to snatch up small reptiles and fish in their long, pincer-like jaws.

▶ **Leaellynasaura**

Water lover
Koolasuchus was a powerful meat-eating **amphibian** from the **Cretaceous Period**. This five-metre-long beast felt at home in fresh water, feeding on fish and other creatures. Now and again, *Koolasuchus* was tempted on to the land. It lay at the water's edge, feeling vibrations in the water with its outsized skull. If a small dinosaur, such as *Leaellynasaura*, stopped to drink, *Koolasuchus* pounced with its teeth-filled jaws wide-open.

▶ **Koolasuchus**

Sea creatures

While dinosaurs and **reptiles** ruled the land during the **Mesozoic Era**, giant marine reptiles ruled the seas. **Plesiosaurs**, **ichthyosaurs** and **mosasaurs** shared the murky waters with fish, turtles, corals and squid. These reptiles had enormous flippers and fins, and, like whales and dolphins today, they had to come to the surface to breathe.

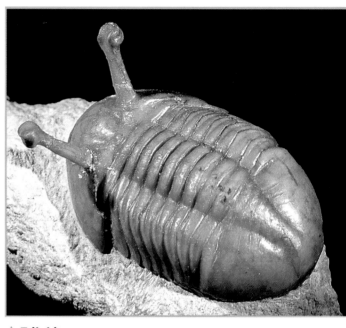

▲ **Trilobites**
One of the earliest animals was the **trilobite**. This ancient relative of crabs, spiders and insects lived on the sea floor 525-250 million years ago. It was one of the first creatures with eyes.

Plesiosaurs

Plesiosaurs, such as *Elasmosaurus*, appeared during the early **Jurassic Period**. These marine giants had long fins, shaped like paddles, which they flapped up and down, flying through the water in the same way that birds fly through the air. Plesiosaurs weren't fast swimmers. Instead, they glided along, waiting for a good moment to open their flat mouths and snap up a fishy meal with their needle-sharp teeth.

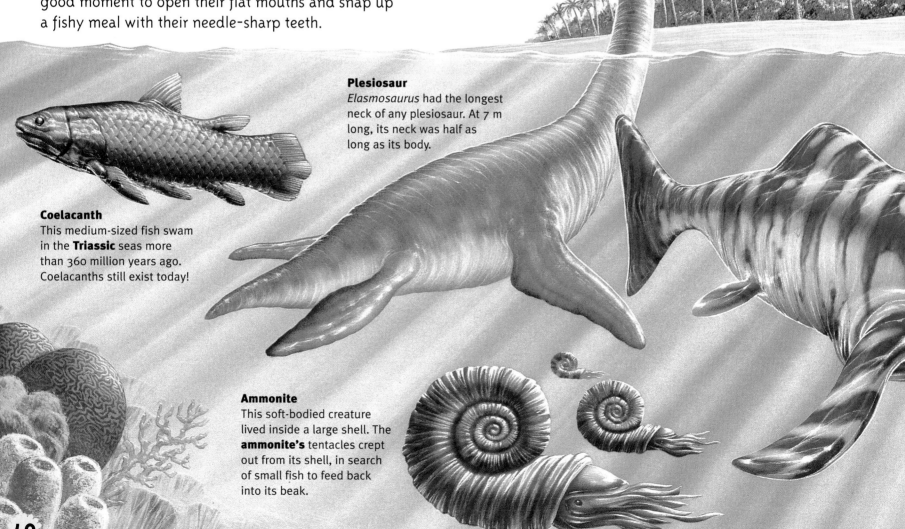

Plesiosaur
Elasmosaurus had the longest neck of any plesiosaur. At 7 m long, its neck was half as long as its body.

Coelacanth
This medium-sized fish swam in the **Triassic** seas more than 360 million years ago. Coelacanths still exist today!

Ammonite
This soft-bodied creature lived inside a large shell. The **ammonite's** tentacles crept out from its shell, in search of small fish to feed back into its beak.

Ichthyosaurs

One group of ocean-going reptiles was the ichthyosaurs, or 'fish-reptiles'. They were speedy swimmers that looked like dolphins and lived off squid, fish and other sea creatures. Ichthyosaurs such as *Ophthalmosaurus* didn't lay eggs, as other reptiles do, but swam close to the surface and gave birth to live young.

WOW!
Liopleurodon was a gigantic plesiosaur. At over 15 m long, it was the biggest carnivore that has ever existed.

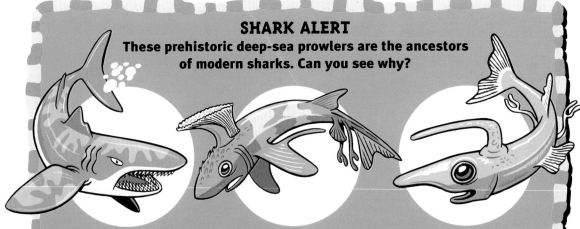

SHARK ALERT
These prehistoric deep-sea prowlers are the ancestors of modern sharks. Can you see why?

Cladoselache cruised the oceans 400 million years ago. This shark was one of the first animals with a backbone to have teeth.

Stethacanthus swam in warm tropical seas 350 million years ago. It had a strange fin on its back, covered with spines that looked like a brush.

Falcatus lived around the same time as *Stethacanthus*. It had a mysterious L-shaped spine on its back that was covered with prickles.

Mosasaurs

Swimming in the warm, sunlit seas of the **Cretaceous Period** were creatures plucked from a sailor's nightmare! A mosasaur such as *Plateocarpus* was fast and powerful, with a huge, eel-like tail that powered it through the water. Like the plesiosaurs, the mosasaurs had paddle fins which they used for steering and turning in the water.

Giant turtle
Archelon was a huge turtle, 4 m across. Like all turtles, *Archelon's* shell formed from ribs that fused together.

Ichthyosaur
Ophthalmosaurus, or 'eye reptile' had enormous eyes which helped it to find squid and fish, its favourite prey.

Mosasaur
Plateocarpus was a large and powerful mosasaur. It could tear ammonites, fish and other sea reptiles apart with its razor-sharp, teeth!

Death of the dinosaurs

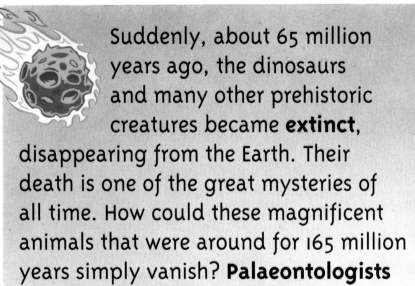

Suddenly, about 65 million years ago, the dinosaurs and many other prehistoric creatures became **extinct**, disappearing from the Earth. Their death is one of the great mysteries of all time. How could these magnificent animals that were around for 165 million years simply vanish? **Palaeontologists** are still trying to solve the case.

▲ **Meteorite crater**
When a meteorite crashes into Earth, it leaves a crater like this. Recently, scientists discovered a crater in Mexico, that is 200 times larger. The meteorite that caused the Mexican crater was large enough to trigger the death of the dinosaurs.

Crashing to Earth

The most popular theory is that a huge rock, called a meteorite, came spinning through space, and collided with the Earth. When the meteorite crashed, a wall of fire spread outwards, burning all the plants and killing dinosaurs for thousands of miles around. When the fires died down, the Earth became extremely cold. Dinosaurs and other **reptiles** couldn't survive the freezing temperatures and died.

Erupting volcanoes

Another theory is that, at the end of the
Cretaceous Period, lots of volcanoes erupted.
Lethal gases from the volcanoes poisoned
many dinosaurs. The volcanoes also threw
mountains of ash and dust into the air,
which blacked out the sun. Without
sunlight, the plants died which meant
that the **herbivores** starved to death.
Then the **carnivores** died because
there weren't any herbivores to eat.

WOW!
One scientist came
up with the mad idea
that dinosaurs died out
because billions of
caterpillars chomped
all the plants on
the planet!

Modern dinosaurs

Although the dinosaurs died out, when
you look up in the air you can still see their
modern descendants — birds. Over millions
of years, the small, two-legged, meat-eating
theropods developed bird-like features
such as feathers and beaks.

Grounded
Mononykus, or 'single claw', was a
flightless bird. It had long legs, a tail,
a short body and really short arms
with claws instead of hands.

Ready for take off
Some scientists think that *Protoavis*
was the first real bird. It had a long
tail and wings with little claws.
Scientists think that *Protoavis* may
have been covered with feathers.

Up, up and away
Other scientists say
that *Archaeopteryx*, the
'ancient wing', was the first
bird. It had hollow bones
and wings, like modern
birds, but it also had sharp
teeth and a bony tail.

Digging for dinosaurs

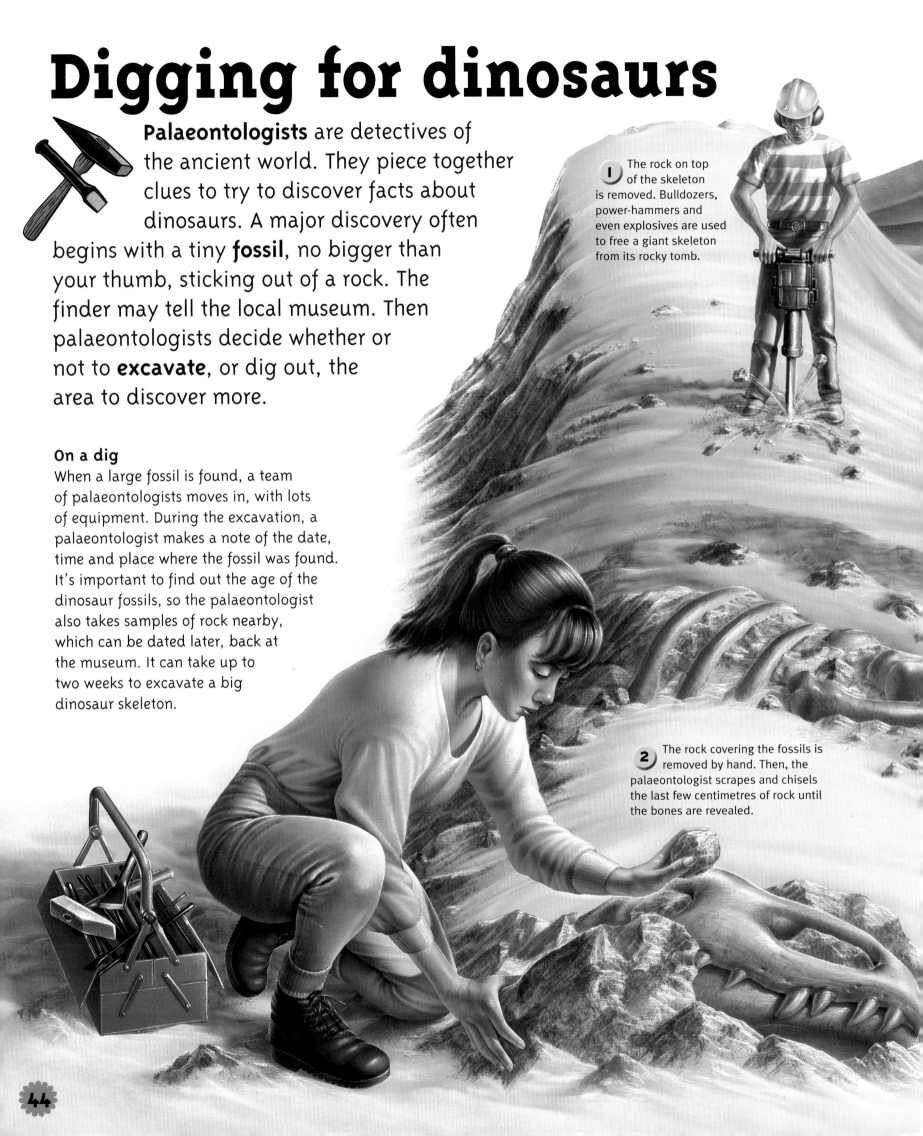

Palaeontologists are detectives of the ancient world. They piece together clues to try to discover facts about dinosaurs. A major discovery often begins with a tiny **fossil**, no bigger than your thumb, sticking out of a rock. The finder may tell the local museum. Then palaeontologists decide whether or not to **excavate**, or dig out, the area to discover more.

On a dig

When a large fossil is found, a team of palaeontologists moves in, with lots of equipment. During the excavation, a palaeontologist makes a note of the date, time and place where the fossil was found. It's important to find out the age of the dinosaur fossils, so the palaeontologist also takes samples of rock nearby, which can be dated later, back at the museum. It can take up to two weeks to excavate a big dinosaur skeleton.

1. The rock on top of the skeleton is removed. Bulldozers, power-hammers and even explosives are used to free a giant skeleton from its rocky tomb.

2. The rock covering the fossils is removed by hand. Then, the palaeontologist scrapes and chisels the last few centimetres of rock until the bones are revealed.

3 The site is mapped out and photographs of the exact positions of the fossils are taken.

4 Small, loose fossil bones are gently brushed and removed from the ground. These fossils are numbered and labelled.

▲ **Palaeontologist at work**
At the local museum, experts, called preparators, carefully remove the last chunks of rock surrounding the fossils. This preparator is chiselling away, to reveal the jaw of a *Tyrannosaurus rex*.

Power tools

Removing a fossil is painstaking work but preparators have lots of tools to help them, from small power-chisels to special powders fired by powerful jets of gas. Often, preparators use vibrating pens with fast-moving tips that eat away hard rock as if it were cheese! One false chip and a whole bone could be lost. This could be a disaster as the bone may be the only one of its type in the world.

UNDERGROUND TO OVERGROUND

Once a dino fossil has been uncovered, the next problem is how to move it. On site, scientists cut away most of the rock around the specimen, leaving the bones on a rocky pedestal that can be moved easily.

Dino fossils may be big but they're not tough. Before the fossils are moved, scientists cover them with layers of tiny pieces of cloth, soaked in plaster of Paris. When the plaster hardens, the ghostly fossil is hauled away.

In the museum, the plaster cast is cracked open. Before the specimen is put on display, the fossils are cleaned and repaired. Then the fossils are filled with a hardening substance, to make them hard-wearing.

Glossary

ammonite An ancient marine animal with a coiled shell that used its tentacles to feed on fish.

amphibian A four-legged animal that can live in or out of water. Frogs, toads and salamanders are amphibians. In the Triassic Period, there were amphibians as large as pigs.

ankylosaur A heavily armoured, four-legged dinosaur with bony plates on its back and a knobbly tail. Ankylosaurs lived during the Cretaceous Period. The word 'ankylosaur' means 'fused reptile'.

atmosphere A layer of gas that surrounds the Earth and protects it from the Sun's rays.

carnivore Any animal with a backbone that kills and eats other backboned animals for food.

ceratopsian A horned dinosaur from the late Cretaceous Period. Ceratopsian means 'horn face'. *Triceratops* and *Centrosaurus* were both ceratopsians.

climate The usual pattern of weather that occurs in a particular place. The climate of a place is similar from year to year. Rainforests, for example, are usually hot and wet.

continent A large area of land on Earth. Today, there are seven continents, but about 210 million years ago, there was only one continent, called Pangaea.

Cretaceous Period The time in Earth's history that lasted from 145 million years ago to 65 million years ago.

excavation A scientific, organized dig, usually for fossils or archaeological remains.

extinction The death, or complete destruction, of a group of animals, or people. The dinosaurs became extinct at the end of the Cretaceous Period.

fossil The ancient remains, or traces, of plants and animals preserved in rock.

gastrolith A stone swallowed by plant-eating dinosaurs that helped to grind up food in their stomachs. Gastrolith means 'stomach stone'.

hadrosaur The scientific name for a dinosaur with a duck-like bill. *Corythosaurus* was a hadrosaur.

herbivore An animal, such as a cow or a sheep, that feeds entirely on plants. Dinosaurs such as *Stegosaurus* and *Apatosaurus* were herbivores.

ichthyosaur An extinct marine reptile that looked similar to a dolphin. Ichthyosaurs hunted fish and squid.

Jurassic Period The time in Earth's history that lasted from 205 million years ago to 145 million years ago.

mammal A warm-blooded animal, with hair or fur, that gives birth to live young and feeds its babies on milk made in its own body. Mammals existed before the dinosaurs.

Mesozoic Era The time from 250 to 65 million years ago, which includes the Triassic, Jurassic and Cretaceous Periods.

migrate To journey from one place to another at the same time every year. Some birds and animals migrate. Dinosaurs also migrated.

▶ **This dinosaur line-up shows how big the dinosaurs were standing beside a man and beside each other.**

man   **Stegosaurus**   **Pachycephalosaurus**   **Euoplocephalus**   **Iguanodon**   **Apatosaurus**

mosasaur A huge marine reptile that lived at the end of the Cretaceous Period. It had a serpent-like body and a long head filled with huge curving teeth.

mya This means 'millions of years ago'.

omnivore Any type of animal, such as a human, bear or bird, that eats plants and other animals. Some dinosaurs were omnivores.

ornithischian This means 'bird-hipped' and it is the scientific name given to dinosaurs with hip bones shaped like those of birds. *Iguanodon* and *Stegosaurus* are examples of ornithischian dinosaurs. All ornithischians were herbivores.

ornithopod A plant-eating dinosaur that walked on either two or four legs. The word 'ornithopod' means 'bird-feet'. *Iguanodon* was an ornithopod. Hadrosaurs, such as *Corythosaurus*, belonged to the ornithopod group too.

pachycephalosaur The name given to a dinosaur with a big, bony domed head, that was used in battle against other dinosaurs. Pachycephalosaur is a scientific word meaning 'thick-headed reptile'.

palaeontologist A scientist who studies fossils. The word 'palaeontologist' means 'those who study ancient life'.

Pangaea Between 270 and 200 million years ago, all the land on Earth was joined into one continent, called Pangaea.

plesiosaur A large marine reptile that lived at the same time as the dinosaurs. Plesiosaurs had short bodies, long necks, four flippers and needle-like teeth.

predator Any animal that hunts, kills and eats other animals for food.

pterosaur A flying reptile that dominated the skies during the Mesozoic Era. Pterosaurs looked like giant bats and some, such as *Pteranodon*, were the size of a small plane.

reptile A cold-blooded animal with scaly skin that lays leathery eggs. Crocodiles, lizards and snakes are all reptiles. Dinosaurs were a special type of reptile.

saurischian This means 'reptile hipped' and it is the name given to dinosaurs with hip bones shaped like those of reptiles. Some saurischians, such as *Tyrannosaurus rex,* were two-legged. Others, like *Diplodocus*, were four-legged.

sauropod A huge, four-legged, long-necked, plant-eating dinosaur, such as *Apatosaurus* or *Mamenchisaurus*. Sauropod means 'reptile feet'.

stegosaur A plant-eating dinosaur with spikes or plates along its back, and spikes at the end of its tail. Stegosaur is a scientific name that means 'roof reptile'.

thecodont A reptile from the Triassic Period. Some thecodonts were armoured plant-eaters. Others were crocodile-like meat-eaters. Scientists believe dinosaurs evolved from this group of animals.

theropod Any two-legged, meat-eating, saurischian dinosaur, such as *Deinonychus* and *Ceratosaurus*. Theropod means 'beast feet'.

Triassic Period The time in Earth's history that lasted from 250 million years ago to 205 million years ago. The very first dinosaurs appeared during the Triassic Period.

trilobite An extinct, segmented animal that lived at the bottom of the sea, feeding on smaller animals. The trilobite was a relative of modern crabs, spiders and insects.

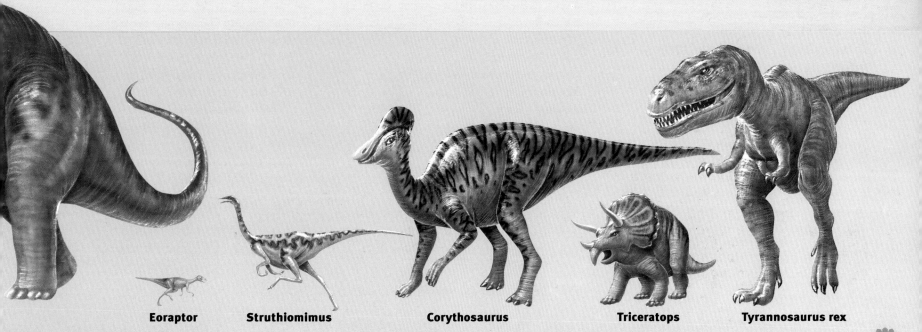

Eoraptor   **Struthiomimus**   **Corythosaurus**   **Triceratops**   **Tyrannosaurus rex**

Index

In this index, the name of each dinosaur is followed by the sounds you need to make to pronounce it properly.